CATFISH PONDS & LILY PADS

Creating and Enjoying a Family Pond

Louise Riotte

A Storey Publishing Book

Storey Communications, Inc.
Schoolhouse Road
Pownal, Vermont 05261

*The mission of Storey Communications
is to serve our customers by publishing practical information
that encourages personal independence in harmony with the environment.*

Edited by Deborah Burns
Cover design by Meredith Maker
Cover illustration by Paul Hoffman
Text design by Susan Bernier
Text production by Jeff Potter, Potter Studio
Line drawings by the author, except on pages 8–9, 11, 31 (lower),
    and 103, by Brigita Fuhrmann
Indexed by Northwind Editorial Services

The information in this book is true and complete to the best of our knowledge. All recommendations are made without guarantee on the part of the author or Storey Communications, Inc. The author and publisher disclaim any liability in connection with the use of this information. For additional information please contact Storey Communications, Inc., Schoolhouse Road, Pownal, Vermont 05261.

Storey Publishing books are available for special premium and promotional uses and for customized editions. For further information, please call the Custom Publishing Department at 800-793-9396.

Printed in the United States by Vicks Lithograph
10 9 8 7 6 5 4 3 2 1

Library of Congress Cataloging-in-Publication Data

Riotte, Louise.
    Catfish ponds and lily pads : creating and enjoying a family pond / Louise Riotte.
        p.   cm.
    "A Storey Publishing Book"
    ISBN 0-88266-949-4 (pbk. : alk. paper)
    1. Fish ponds — Design and construction.   2. Water gardens — Design and construction.
    3. Fish ponds — Oklahoma — Design and construction — Anecdotes.   4. Water gardens
    — Oklahoma — Design and construction — Anecdotes.   5. Riotte, Louise.   I. Title.
SH157.85.F52R46
639'.8—dc20   96-41127
                                                                                CIP

Table of Contents

PREFACE

JUST THINK OF the advantages of having a pond of your very own providing so much tranquility and fishing pleasure. On holidays you don't need to drive 50 or 100 miles and then compete with others at an overcrowded lake. You can just saunter down to your own favorite spot. Catch enough fish for a family lunch, dress them out, prepare them for the table, and have a feast of fresh fish that a king would envy. Forgive me for waxing eloquent. I am just so full of enthusiasm that I get carried away. I can't help myself! Building a pond, watching it fill, and dreaming of the day you will be fishing in it — this is an exciting adventure.

This is an idea book, a sort of "wake up and see the possibilities of all these things that you might like to see, or do, or profit by." Because regulations and conditions vary all over the country, *it is essential that you contact your local and state authorities for guidance before building your own pond.* Your local and state laws and soil and water conditions may be very different from ours in Oklahoma.

When our land was young and untouched, there was so much abundance to be had simply for the taking. Unlike now, there were few laws to protect certain species and the environment as a whole. And so sometimes we are apt to think, "There's nothing left for me." But there is! It's just that now things are a little more complicated. You have to know the rules and obey the laws — necessary because certain species would vanish from the earth if they were not protected.

There is still an abundance of fish, streams and manmade lakes are regularly stocked, and the fishing environment is wonderful. All you need are your license and a copy of the rules giving limits on each species and you are on your way. You can still catch fish just as people did a hundred or so years ago and have all the fun of reeling them in just as they did.

If you are fortunate enough to have a private pond you can raise the fish of your choice and catch them for a feast whenever you want to. You have stocked your pond with fish, fed them, cared for them, and they are as much yours as a flock of chickens! Only common sense rules apply. This is also true of the bullfrogs, turtles, crayfish, and snails that may arrive spontaneously.

Life is full of other pleasures and possibilities as well. Pearl-bearing mussels still exist in the waters of the Mississippi and in unpolluted lakes and streams. You just have to search a little harder to find them. Gemstones and semiprecious stones are still to be found, free as in Rockhound State Park in New Mexico, or hunted for a small fee, as are diamonds in Arkansas. Don't forget about fossil hunting, when you're excavating for your pond or if you vacation in a likely spot.

Enjoy barbecued or smoked fish in the Southwest, a clambake in New England, or fresh pan-fried rainbow trout in the North. Catch grunion with your hands on a Southern California beach and cook them right there for some of the most delicious eating you have ever enjoyed. Kids under sixteen can catch them free; adults need a state license.

All through most of my eighty-eight years I have enjoyed all these wonderful things, and my wish for you is that you may also live a long and happy life and enjoy them as well.

Louise Riotte

PART ONE

Creating a Pond

Chapter 1

BUILDING OUR
DREAM POND

OUR LOVE AFFAIR with pond building began when we fell into our first pond — literally! And, at the time, it was completely dry!

I had accompanied my son, Eugene, and his family to church on a Sunday morning. We had planned to look over a small acreage afterward that he was considering for purchase as a possible building site for a new and larger home. The area had not been mowed, and was covered with beautiful wildflowers indigenous to southern Oklahoma — violet-blue lupines, Indian paintbrush, spring beauties, white daisies, and purple coneflowers. There was also a nice variety of native pecan, red cedar, and several species of large native oak.

Birds were singing, butterflies were flitting about, and I guess we were just carried away by all that natural beauty, along with the invigorating freshness of the springtime air and the perfect clarity of the blue, cloudless sky. We were so excited we just didn't watch where we were going. And johnsongrass and wild sunflowers, which obscured the ravine, grow very tall in southern Oklahoma.

The snowy egret enjoys our pond almost as much as we do.

Suddenly we found ourselves tumbling down a gentle incline. Our fall was broken by clumps of grass. Luckily none of us was injured. Laughing, we picked ourselves up and found that we were in a deep area that had been obscured by the tall grasses. We were already in love with the beautiful acreage but now realized there was a serious problem. Filling in that big, deep ravine would be very expensive.

My son was not completely depressed, however, and decided to talk to the property owner the following day, using our discovery for leverage to see if the price might be lowered. He found upon inquiry that the location could indeed be had for an attractive price, as it had been passed over many times by prospective purchasers for the same reason that we found troubling.

He bought the lot. Thereafter, he wore such a smug expression that friends who drove out to see it after it had been mowed could not resist teasing him about his big hole in the ground. He bore it all with good-natured patience, saying nothing. (Later they would say, "Why didn't I think of that?")

The "hole in the ground" was situated in the approximate center of his land but fairly close to the northern edge, so there was a larger space to the south of it. There his lovely brick home was built, with a large picture window carefully placed so the "hole" could be viewed from the dining area. While this was going on, he really was subjected to some very colorful comments. But his best friend, a man of about his own age, wasn't laughing.

Eugene had consulted with him before making his purchase and they were soon working together on a possible solution that did not involve *filling in* but rather *digging out* to *deepen*. Eugene's friend, a cattle rancher and owner of several hundred acres, had some five to ten well-built ponds on his ranch, initially constructed for watering the cattle but now also well stocked with catfish. We were privileged to fish on the ranch whenever we wished, but the ranch was some distance away and my son had simply decided that he would like to have a well-stocked pond of his own.

At the time Oklahoma — especially southern Oklahoma — was still in the middle of the oil boom, and there weren't many bulldozer operators in the area. It was decided to use the person who had built our friend's ranch ponds. This involved some unexpected problems. Our friend was working at the time with an Alcoholics Anonymous rehabilitation program and made a point of helping the members find employment. He had used this 'dozer operator a number of times on his own property with excellent results. The man knew his trade well, but because of his drinking problem was notably unreliable. Employment in the oil fields, at that time, paid more than bulldozing. After we looked around for a bit, he seemed to be about all there was to choose from, so he was hired . . . on a Monday.

He worked with due diligence all week but disappeared on Saturday, and it was then that we found out that he was serving out a sentence in the local jail for having a fight while "in his cups" the week before in a local tavern. He was mild-mannered and efficient when sober, but "the sauce" changed his personality and he became belligerent. We had a situation reminiscent of the TV series *Mayberry RFD* in which Sheriff Andy Taylor had to lock up the gentle Otis on weekends. Our compassionate local chief of police permitted our employee to work during the week so he could support his family and had him "do time" on weekends.

The weather cooperated that spring, and the pond building went well. Along about this time a funny incident occurred. Since my son had a business to attend to, he couldn't oversee the pond operations. Our rancher friend agreed to do this, dropping by from time to time to make sure all was going according to plan. This involved, among other things, dropping a plumb line at intervals to see when the desired depth had been reached. We attached the line to the end of a long fishing pole.

Another workman on the property was clearing out underbrush. Watching the man in the big Stetson and cowboy boots who was walking around the excavation, he became deeply concerned. Eventually, he could stand it no longer. He jumped in his pickup, raced into town, and pulled up at Eugene's place of business. He rushed in shouting, "Gene, Gene, there's a crazy man out at your house, he's been trying to fish all morning in a dry hole. You'd better come out and see what's going on!"

My son, at first surprised, soon understood what was happening and set matters straight — when he finally stopped laughing.

Even before the pond was completed, water had begun to accumulate in the deepest portion. Our operator, experienced in such situations, continued to work as soon as weather permitted and went on to completion. As rain continued to fall, we watched anxiously to see how well the pond would hold the water. We were very pleased. During the cool fall months, little evaporation took place and the water level remained almost constant.

My son's acreage is situated to the far south of Oklahoma. It is below the foothills of the Arbuckles (with beautiful Turner Falls just to the north) and this affects our climate, making it much warmer than the northern part of our state. We are said to have more sunny days than even sunny California and this I believe. We are so close to the border of North Texas that we tend to have much the same weather and about the same rainfall.

This area, comprising Ardmore, Oklahoma, and the Texas cities of Sherman and Denison, is known as "Texoma" — and we share pretty much the same weather reports.

Our operator, in building the pond, made use of the tributary of Pecan Creek (usually dry in the summer but providing excellent run-off in the spring months). The counties to the north of us received even more rain and this brought a good flow of water into Pecan Creek, which eventually wended its way to our pond. The pond water, during the filling process, was still unsettled and took on the hue of reddish-yellow, the color of the clay in which it is built.

Natural Air Conditioning

One of the biggest advantages of a pond is the effect on temperature of the surrounding area, tending to make it more even, that is, it is warmer in the winter and cooler in the summer. Trees, too, according to George ("Doc") Abraham affect, the immediate climate, acting as natural air conditioners. They also act as "dust mops," catching much of the falling particles found in the 12 million tons of pollutants released into the atmosphere above the United States each year. The hairy surfaces of plant leaves on trees, bushes, grass, vines, and all other plants catch the particles from the air. Then, with rainfall, the pollutants are washed into the soil, where they are no longer a danger to man's breathing apparatus. Gardening of all types improves the environment. According to "Doc" a tree near your home can produce a cooling effect equal to 10 room-size air conditioners running 20 hours a day. And an acre of grass in front of your home gives off 2,400 gallons of precious water every hot summer day.

So the pond was built. By late spring it was becoming very hot indeed — not just warm but *hot*. I mean *hot!* Grass around the pond began to turn yellow and small cracks appeared in the dam and we were very concerned. It was a heck of a day — 100 degrees at noon — to set out Bermuda grass on the pond's shoulders but this hardy plant can stand just about anything. Early in the morning we had taken the trailer to a nursery about 25 miles away and loaded it down with freshly cut swaths about 2 by 4 feet. These were placed at intervals around the shoulders of the dam, pressed in freshly disturbed shallow areas, and covered lightly

A Problem Solved

On Mother's Day I took the "grand tour." Since I find walking painful now, at my age, I traveled on the riding lawn mower with Laura Elizabeth on one side and my son on the other. First we visited the orchard of fruit and nut trees and then went on to the pond. A problem had arisen — literally! Apparently the increase of water in the pond had caused the large truck tires to surface due to the air still contained in them. We solved this dilemma in typical Western style, by shooting the tires. Using a large caliber shotgun, we shot holes in the tires, puncturing them sufficiently for the air to be let out. They sank again to their appointed places, awaiting the day when papa catfish would use them for breeding. Problem solved. Learn by our mistake and bore large holes in the tires to let the air out *before* you place them in your pond.

When we returned to the house, Joan, my daughter-in-law, had prepared a wonderful lunch of barbecued pork ribs, baked sweet potatoes, broccoli, salad and green onions from our own gardens — followed by strawberry shortcake. I had a great Mother's Day.

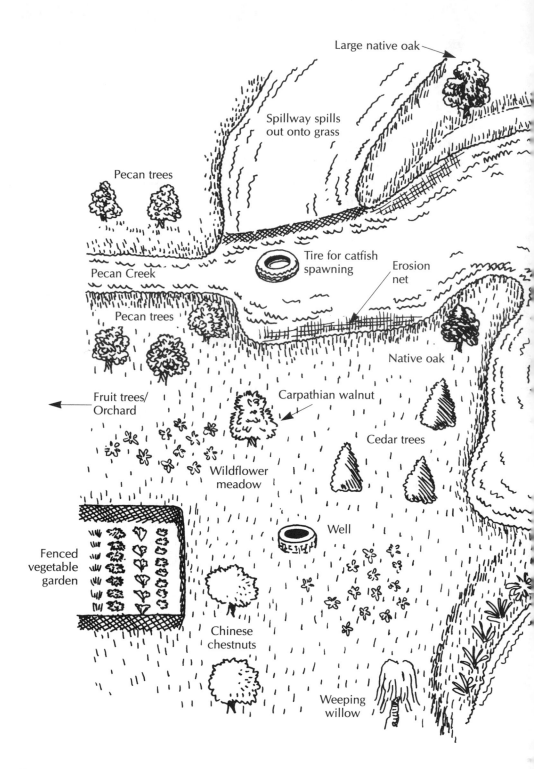

Large native oak

Spillway spills out onto grass

Pecan trees

Pecan Creek

Tire for catfish spawning

Erosion net

Pecan trees

Native oak

Fruit trees/ Orchard

Carpathian walnut

Cedar trees

Wildflower meadow

Well

Fenced vegetable garden

Chinese chestnuts

Weeping willow

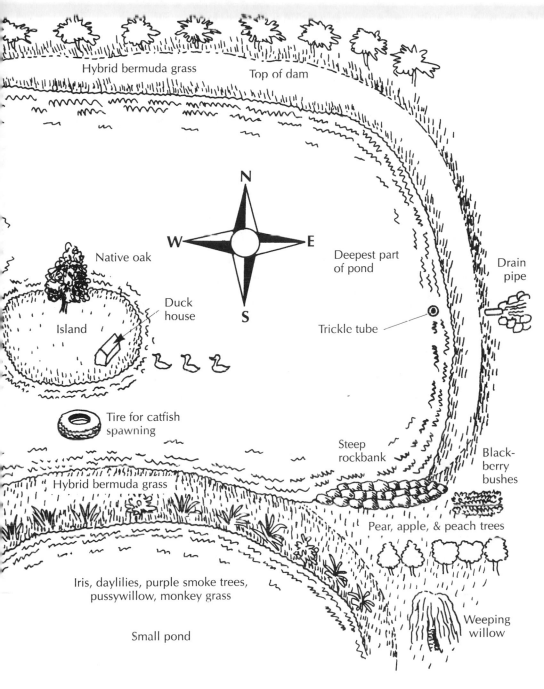

Hybrid bermuda grass

Top of dam

Native oak

Island

Duck house

Deepest part of pond

Drain pipe

Trickle tube

Tire for catfish spawning

Steep rockbank

Black-berry bushes

Hybrid bermuda grass

Pear, apple, & peach trees

Iris, daylilies, purple smoke trees, pussywillow, monkey grass

Small pond

Weeping willow

A map of our pond.

with good soil. It was my job to follow this operation and do the watering. A good rain a few days later assured their growth, and the runoff added a considerable amount of water to the pond.

I am curiously afflicted! I never can stand to look at a bare spot without wanting to plant something. Accordingly, a few days later I looked over the profusion of plant life in my own yard. I decided that the iris, daylilies, tulips, monkey grass, and a few other things needed dividing and set about digging a trailerload for planting the perimeter of the pond. It was hard work and I wore a sunbonnet, dark glasses, and protective clothing as well as some sunscreen when I set about my self-appointed task — a labor of love.

The soil was uncooperative — hard, cloddy clay. The same soil that was ideal for holding the water in the pond was like a rock by the middle of summer. Nevertheless, I persisted and eventually, over a period of days, got everything in, mixing some good sandy loam and peat moss to give cover to the plants. Everything lived and we were later to add several weeping willows, pussy willows, purple smoke plants, and forsythia. The rewards were ample — in the spring, seen from the dining area, the pond and its plantings look like fairyland.

The ideas did not end there. My son, after the passage of enough time to build up his financial resources again, decided it would be prudent — and he would be assured of more privacy — to buy additional acreage. Accordingly, he purchased land to the west of his original property and to the north. A road on the east prevented additional purchase there.

The western acreage and selected portions of his original property were to become his orchard and garden. Having long since used up all the available space on my own land, I planned to give him carefully selected fruit and nut trees for birthday and Christmas gifts, along with 200 shade trees from the Oklahoma Forestry Division (see *Sources)*. We'd plant these on the perimeter of his property for a windbreak and erosion-control program.

I think it might be interesting to mention here that just about any kind of nut tree will grow in southern Oklahoma — black walnut, butternut, Carpathian walnut, chestnut (Chinese) — especially beautiful — and even almonds (which will bear about as often as their relative, the peach, in favorable years — those that don't have a late freeze at the time of blossoming). Grafted pecans of several varieties are also valuable additions. I have written of the culture of these in my book *The Complete Guide to Growing Nuts* (see *Sources*).

The property to the north became our second and much larger pond. I would like to tell you about our experience and how to apply what we did — and sometimes what we should have done — to your own situation.

Below is a diagram of one kind of dam. Be sure to check with your local authorities to find out what kind of dam is suitable for your area and for the pond you're planning.

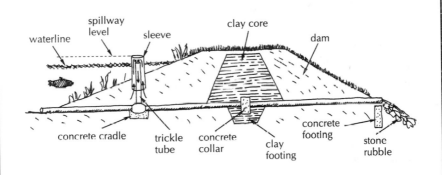

A cross-section of a dam.

Chapter 2

GETTING STARTED

OUR FIRST "sky pond" came about, at least partially, as a way of solving a problem of the contours of the land. But our second one was planned for quite a different reason. In recent years, the pollution of many rivers, smaller streams, and lakes is rapidly becoming more and more of a health hazard. It is increasingly difficult to be sure that the waters you are fishing in are sufficiently clean and pure. Having your own pond will give you control over this and add to both your fishing and eating pleasure.

A pond takes space, but even a large lot will accommodate one of modest proportions if there are no building restrictions. Of course, the nicest thing about a pond is its beauty, in all seasons. It offers an opportunity to develop the loveliest spot on your property and will provide an interesting area for picnics and family fun even in its initial stages of development.

If you are already the owner of some property, you will, of course, need to work within the framework of what's possible. If you are con-

By creating a pond you are doing a favor for the wildlife in your area

templating the purchase of a building site, the information contained in this chapter may be even more helpful.

In writing this book I am endeavoring to give as much information as possible, but there are essential limitations of time and space. Much of what I write must be of a general nature, for pond size and type of fish to be cultured will necessarily vary. Some of my readers may simply wish to have a small pond for family use with friends occasionally invited, or the intent may be for commercial growing. Or maybe both — a small pond may lead to a larger one and eventually to commercial fish farming. There is a growing demand for fish by the health-conscious, and many restaurants nowadays are specializing in fish dishes.

John W. Jensen, of the Alabama Cooperative Extension Service, Southern Regional Aquaculture Center (see *Sources*), has written extensively and informatively on pond site selection and construction. Much of what he has to say will apply to other parts of the country with the proviso that in colder sections it might be advisable to deepen at least a portion of the pond area to allow the fish to go down when the pond freezes over.

According to Jensen, pond site selection and design may be the most important factors determining the success of aquaculture, whether for private use or for profit. Ponds that leak, have irregular bottoms, or suffer from routine water shortages will not produce abundant crops of fish.

Take a Look at Your Property

A house or a lot on which you plan to build is a big investment — perhaps the largest you'll make during your lifetime — and you can't afford to make mistakes. Unsuspected soil hazards, not discernible from the surface, can cause serious damage and lead to major expense. Soil surveys, available from the Soil Conservation Service (see *Sources*), can help answer many questions about your proposed homesite before you build or buy.

Is Your Home on a Floodplain?

For instance, some home buyers don't realize that their home is on flood-prone land until it's too late. Many areas now used for houses were farms, woodlots, and pasture just a few years ago. Some of these are on the floodplain of a stream — a stream that may not be apparent except in a period of unusually heavy rainfall. I have in mind a spot just north of one of our large supermarkets, a low place in the paved street that is subject to flash flooding. On several occasions cars have been swept off the road and the people in them have drowned.

A stream near your homesite may overflow only once in 5 or 10 years, but the chance of eventual damage is great and may get greater as more development takes place in the upstream drainage area. Many people do not realize that even the tributary of a small creek can become a raging, destructive torrent following prolonged or heavy rains.

In many parts of the country, people whose homes have been severely damaged by floods were not aware that their houses were built on a floodplain. Because about 5 percent of the land in the United States is on floodplains and much of this land is level and seemingly desirable for home building, a prospective home buyer should determine whether flooding is a hazard. Soil surveys show the extent of flood-prone areas and indicate the problem of flooding on soils there.

A seasonally high water table is a hazard in many areas. The water may be at a safe depth for most of the year but rise during the wet season. If the water table rises close to the surface, basements could be flooded, septic tank absorption fields may fail, and plants may be damaged or killed. Unfortunately, you can't tell about the water table just by walking over the site. Soil surveys indicate whether soils have a seasonally high water table.

This situation can also endanger a fish pond, bringing in toxic wastes and causing water pollution — the very thing you are trying to avoid.

Most floodplains have been mapped. I obtained a map called "City of Ardmore, Oklahoma, Carter County" from the Federal Emergency Management Agency, Flood Map Distribution Center (see *Sources*), and similar maps are obtainable for other areas. This one gave me some very interesting information that I had never dreamed of, including the names of many small streams and their tributaries that actually run through our little city. I had often wondered why, almost every spring, certain low-lying areas were flooded. Looking over the map I found that tributaries of Pecan Creek, Hickory Creek, Sandy Creek, Caddo Creek, Anadarche Creek, and others were all right there wending their way through both the residential and business areas. Reading the map was a most enlightening experience.

Working with the Natural Topography

Topography will determine the size and shape of a watershed pond. Generally, steep slopes in V-shaped valleys require larger-volume dams per water surface acre than will sites with gently sloping hills and wide, flat valleys. Building a pond in steep terrain costs more per pond acre than do ponds built in gently rolling terrain.

I think our second pond, of approximately one acre, might best be described as being built in gently rolling terrain. We wanted it to be irregular in shape for attractiveness and also so an island could be constructed to save a particularly large and beautiful native oak with possum grapes festooning its branches. The island is intended to serve another purpose; it is the home of our flock of white ducks and African geese, affording them some protection from the coyotes and bobcats that come in from the nearby woods. Wild ducks and Canada geese often join our domestic variety in our first pond. Occasionally, we catch a glimpse of the gorgeous plumage of a pheasant among the trees. Not so welcome are the armadillos, which have wended their way up from Texas.

Ideally, watershed ponds should be less than 10 feet deep at the dam. Deeper ponds must be partially drained for a clean harvest. Our bulldozer operator advised us to go no deeper than 8 feet, which is all right in southern Oklahoma, where ponds almost never freeze. In more northern climates, a little deeper is desirable.

Gently sloping topography allows for two-sided and three-sided watershed ponds constructed parallel to hills bordering a creek. Runoff is used as a water source but a dam does not cross a hollow or a draw. Objectives in building these ponds are to avoid large, uncontrolled waterways and to make them seinable without draining in order to harvest.

Select sites so that pipes and valves can be installed to drain the pond completely. Floods from nearby rivers should not overflow the dam, and floods within the watershed should not endanger the structure. Information on the 100-year flood potential is available from district offices of the U.S. Soil Conservation Service.

Mark off the waterline of the proposed pond to make sure that water does not encroach on properties owned by others. If the area is classified as a wetland, the U.S. Army Corps of Engineers, and possibly some state agencies, will require a permit before construction begins. Contact your local county Extension agent about other possible restrictions.

Soil surveys of counties throughout the United States are published by the Soil Conservation Service in cooperation with state and federal agencies. Each survey has maps that show the location of each kind of soil in its area. This is of importance in pond building, as some soils have a greater or lesser capacity for holding water. The maps include descriptions of soils and rate their limitations for many uses. By identifying the soil area in which your homesite is situated, and by reading the description of the soil, you can determine what hazards, if any, may affect the site.

A soil survey is helpful to give clues to general soil types in the area. However, test pits should be dug to get a more accurate reading.

In our area, good quality soil containing at least 20 percent clay is necessary for building dams and spillways. (Ours contains slightly more than 20 percent clay.) This includes clay, silty clay, and sandy clay soils. Soils should be sampled by frequent borings along a proposed dam site to check for a clay base. A back hoe is even better for test pits, as it exposes a more accurate cross-section of the soil structure.

In other parts of the country it is not considered necessary to have 20 percent clay soil. Silt and fine sand will compact and make a waterproof dam. Check with professionals in your area.

In our case our Kubota tractor, which has an attachment called a "tree auger," was very useful for this purpose. It is also good for digging holes for fence posts, and we used it for planting an additional 200 trees purchased from the state forestry division around the perimeter of the pond for purposes of erosion control. These were 50 loblolly pine, 50 Austrian pine, 50 baldcypress and 50 black locust. Because of its fibrous roots black locust is especially useful, as well as being exceptionally beautiful. Black locust trees have panicles of white, delightfully scented flowers in the spring, beloved of our honeybees. Cost of trees and shipment, $57.50.

Borings for additional clay sources should be taken in the vicinity of the dam. If removal of clay from the pond bottom uncovers rock formations, sand, or gravel areas, it is best to leave the clay in place.

Pond construction in limestone areas can be especially risky because of underlying cracks and sinks, which may cause ponds to leak. In limestone areas soils should be bored to check for soil quality in the area to be covered by water. Approximately 4 borings per acre are sufficient unless there are soil type variations in the pond bottom.

Other Problems

When we began construction on our second pond, we discovered another problem that had been hidden by extensive undergrowth. Some previous owner had dumped what appeared to be the concrete foundations of a building into a heap. We exterminated the inhabitants — snakes, including some rattlers — but were still left with the disposal problem. We took a different approach and instead of removal, we mixed cement and completely covered the area, thus preventing possible leakage. Under normal conditions, however, all debris should be removed from the site to prevent possible future problems.

A soil survey map can also help you determine whether or not you are going to strike bedrock 5 feet down — and entirely defeat your wonderful idea of building a dream pond — or if the land is a former garbage dump that has been filled in to be sold as a site for home building! What about toxic waste? Or something even stranger and more unusual?

When our family moved out to Oklahoma from Kentucky, my father bought a lovely, rambling old house, charmingly situated on a gently rolling hill. The 10-foot ceilings in a day of no air conditioning made it cool and comfortable. He had been amazed at the unbelievably low price for such a handsome structure with ample surrounding land, fertile and intensely green and full of beautiful wildflowers.

Shortly after we moved in, we began hearing puzzling rumors. As we made friends, an occasionally disquieting phrase or word would be introduced into the conversation. Eventually people could not resist telling my mother the history of our homesite. Acquaintances, with glittering eyes and hugely enjoying themselves as they watched for her reaction, would ask, "Did you know your house is on an Indian burial ground?" My mother, sturdy of mind and always a lady, would smile gently and reply, "Yes, indeed, but I have never feared the dead; it's the living I'm sometimes frightened of."

She had a right to be. At that stage of development, before statehood, Oklahoma was a dumping ground for many men with a lurid past. Wanted elsewhere, they could hide out in Oklahoma's caverns and woodlands. (Devil's Den, near Tishomingo, was a favorite place.) Many of them were once wealthy, now bitter, displaced Southerners, men who had lost everything but their good manners! Many were the tales of robberies of banks and stagecoaches by polite bandits who said "Please" and "Thank you" as they set about their nefarious deeds.

She was also right about not fearing the dead. My mother soon made friends with the Indians. Her knowledge of herbalism was highly respected, especially by the medicine men, who called her *Hilleah-ta-ha,* meaning "One-Who-Thinks-Good."

There were no apparitions, clanking chains, or screams in the night. Those who slept there did so peacefully. In time my mother planted fruit trees, made a garden, and grew flowers, and created a special garden for cooking and medicinal herbs.

Her peaches bore bushels; her apples were large, red-cheeked, and delicious; her grapes were bursting with honeyed sweetness. Her flowers always seemed to be larger, brighter, and more profuse than those of her friends. Her rose gardens were famous throughout the territory.

In good physical and mental health right to the last, she lived to the grand old age of 93.

Perhaps . . . there *was* a manifestation after all — and we were blessed.

Once, digging to plant a new rosebush, I found a tiny white china doll about 2 inches high. It was by no means a work of art, having rough edges and facial features slightly blurred. It looked as if it might have been produced in a mold. I have always loved the Native American people and it was very precious to me, as I believed it might have been the treasured possession of a little Indian girl of long ago. I still have it. Some of these dolls were only an inch high.

In later years I learned that these dolls were widely used as "trade goods," along with beads and the big iron kettles the Indians wanted for cooking *pashofa,* which was both the name of the food (pork and hominy cooked together at festivals) and the name of the gathering.

Water

There are three sources of water: surface water (springs, streams, and reservoirs), groundwater (wells), and watershed runoff. Some ponds draw from a combination of these.

Levee Ponds

If yours will be a levee pond, built on flat land and filled with ground water or surface water, it will be perfectly suitable for producing fish. The water for filling this kind of pond should come from a well, spring, reservoir, or stream, since there will be no runoff water. The best choice is a well or a spring. Streams and reservoirs have erratic water levels, unreliable water quality and, sometimes, wild fish that can enter your pond and cause management problems.

Keep in mind that in many areas of the country it is not recommended to drill wells just to maintain a pond. Such wells many times are pumped dry. Springs, groundwater, and watershed runoff are preferable for filling a pond.

Water Witching

In southern Oklahoma, rainfall is often scanty, especially during the summer months. We solved our water problems by drilling two deep water wells.

Here it is interesting to note that the drilling site for both of our wells was determined by "water witching," using willow wands from our own trees. Water witching, sometimes called dowsing, whose proper name is *radiesthesia,* may be an inherited ability. I am a water witch, my son is a water witch, and so is his daughter. That's how it goes. Our driller was also a water witch and so are many others who may not be aware of possessing this ability. Each of us used the willow wand and came within a foot or two of each other. Later in the day another friend and neighbor, Jess Cook, also traced the vein using a willow switch and reached the same conclusion. This test took place on a Sunday in September.

The following Tuesday, Jim Donham, of Donham Drilling Company, drilled a test hole. He found nothing until he passed into an extremely hard sandstone formation at 155 feet. He struck water at this depth in such abundance that he went 30 feet deeper, still in the formation, setting perforated casing, believing he had struck an underground river. He is a driller of many years' experience and he told us he had drilled only two other wells of equal capacity. This well has never pumped dry.

The well delivered approximately 100 gallons a minute of clean, very cold, good-tasting water, with no trace of iron or salt. It was tested at the Noble Foundation (see *Sources*). Jim told us that only one well out of a hundred is likely to be this good.

The next Saturday his compay installed a 1½-hp Red Jacket pump, dug a ditch, and laid an electric line. The pump began working at approximately 5:30 P.M. The first water was slightly muddy but quickly cleared. The water was allowed to flow into the adjacent pond (our first) and left on flow all night and all day. Still flowing, the well ran for 48 hours (5:30 Saturday to 5:30 Monday) and the flow did not diminish. Flow estimate through the garden hose was 30 gallons per minute.

Donham Drilling Company drilled a second well in our newly acquired west field area near the gate and reached water at 220 feet. As with the previous well, the water was tested at the Noble Foundation and found to contain no detrimental material. It was also suitable for drinking purposes as well as agricultural use. We use both wells for watering garden, fruit and nut trees, lawn, and pond when needed. We note that this water promotes plant growth faster and more abundantly than the water from our "city" source.

If you plan a pond in hilly terrain, you can take advantage of runoff from rainfall on the watershed. Dams are constructed across valleys, to form reservoirs where the runoff water is stored.

Watershed Ponds

In rolling or hilly areas, water to fill and maintain a pond may come entirely from watershed runoff, although groundwater and surface water can be used to supplement it. In building our second, larger pond our bulldozer operator made good use of a small tributary of Pecan Creek running through my son's land on the northern portion. Dry in the hot, windy summer, it provides excellent runoff with the spring rains.

It is desirable that the watershed-to-water-surface-acreage ratio should be large enough to fill a pond during the rainy months but allow it to drop no more than 2 feet during drier periods. The ratio varies from 5 acres of land for each surface acre of pond in heavy clay soil on open sites to 30 acres or more for each surface acre of pond on porous, wooded sites.

When a watershed is too small to supply enough water to the pond, an outside source (wells, streams, or rivers — in our case, wells) is needed. Check your state and local regulations, however, before using these sources. When ponds are built in series in a valley, less watershed is needed to maintain a pond. Before harvest, water can be pumped or drained from one pond to another for storage. This allows ponds to be refilled, using the stored water, immediately after harvest.

Water quality is affected by the watershed. Waters of low alkalinity generally originate from acid soils. Alkaline water (50 to 300 ppm of $CaCO_3$) is the most desirable for fish production. Neutralize acid pond soils with applications of agricultural limestone.

The biggest disadvantage of watershed ponds is erratic water supply. In many areas of the country, dependable rain for filling ponds occurs only during winter and early spring. Because fish are often inventoried and/or grown until late spring or summer, draining for harvest then may result in the loss of production.

Law Enforcement and the Pond

As with just about everything, there are rules. I can give you general guidelines but these regulations vary from state to state. Rules also change over time as we learn more about the effect our activities have on the environment. You should check out your plans with your own state if you contemplate building a pond for either recreational or commercial use.

What Is a Private Pond?

To understand the rules that apply to ponds, one first must understand the legal definition of a private pond. To be considered a truly private pond, a water body must be constructed rather than natural, and it must be located entirely on the property of only one landowner or lessee.

Except during floods, the private pond must have no connection with streams or other bodies of water that would allow the passage of fish between the two locations. The private pond may, however, be connected with a stream or other body of water by a pipe no larger than 8 inches in diameter if it is screened to prevent the movement of fish between the two locations. To be deemed a private pond, it cannot have been stocked with fish provided by the Department of Wildlife and Parks within the last 10 years. Once stocked by the Department of Wildlife and Parks, a pond loses its private impoundment status for a decade.

Fishing Regulations

No one needs a state fishing license to fish in a private pond. On all other ponds (we'll call them "non-private ponds"), however, only certain persons are exempt from the license requirement. The landowner or tenant and family members living in residence may fish a non-private pond without a fishing license. In general, residents on leave from active duty in the armed forces, residents under 16 years of age or over 65, and non-residents under 16 are not required to have a license. Everyone else must have a license in possession.

Both private and non-private ponds are open to fishing year-round. On those impoundments legally qualifying as private ponds, no daily creel or possession limits apply. On non-private ponds such as those stocked by the Department of Wildlife and Parks within the past 10 years, the limits established by regulation apply. No bass length limits are in effect on private or non-private ponds, other than those imposed by the pond owner.

Lawful fishing methods vary according to the pond's status. Anyone may take fish from a private pond by any means except those using a substance that could escape or endanger or kill fish in other waters. On non-private ponds, all anglers — including the owner and tenants — may take fish only by methods established by regulation. A landowner, a tenant, and other anglers could thus take fish by seining a private pond, but no one could use this method on a non-private pond.

Fossils and Gem Stones

While excavating your pond, be aware of the possibilities of discovery. Fossils are often found surprisingly near the surface, appearing after heavy rains. An Indiana couple recently found some mastodon bones while digging their fishing pond. You may make a find of historical importance or detect the presence of gems and semiprecious stones deeper down. And it could be profitable to check the clear, shallow beds of streams and tributaries that flow into your pond for both fossils and semiprecious gems. Flowing water often brings such treasures to the surface, and they are more apparent when wet. I found a lovely, rounded stone of rose quartz in Pecan Creek. Cut, shaped, and polished, it became two exquisite, rosy cabochons — one for me and one for Laura Elizabeth, my granddaughter.

At one time it was my privilege to be secretary to Dr. Charles Weldon Tomlinson. Dr. Tomlinson had been a Geology Professor at Columbia University but retired to become an independent oil operator in southern Oklahoma. Dr. Tomlinson and his wife, who was also a geologist, took my husband and me on many field trips to study rock formations. Dr. Maynard White, paleontologist, whose specialty was fossils, often accompanied us.

Oklahoma was, in ages past, part of an inland sea. The climate was tropical and the vegetation contributed to the immense oil reserves of the state. Dinosaur bones have been found here. Several weeks ago a farmer, plowing his field, was astonished to come across an almost complete skeleton.

The landowner or tenant may raise fish for commercial use in a private pond, but sale of fish from non-private ponds is prohibited. The taking of bullfrogs from ponds is also regulated. The license requirements, open season dates, lawful methods, and daily limits are exactly the same for both private and non-private ponds and public waters.

Access

Any landowner or tenant has the right to restrict access to a pond on his land regardless of whether the pond is private or non-private. One who enters onto another's property without permission is violating the law. Just because the Department of Wildlife and Parks has stocked a pond or it doesn't qualify as private according to the legal definition doesn't mean a landowner can't regulate who uses his property. The only exception is that for ponds over 20 acres to receive a full allotment from the Department of Wildlife and Parks, the owner must sign an agreement that states he will allow access to persons who ask permission to fish one year after fish are stocked and for nine years thereafter. The pond owner has the right to refuse access to anyone who previously destroyed property or exhibited other undesirable behavior.

The Law Enforcement Officer

State conservation officers and other law enforcement officials have the right to enter upon private property in the performance of their duties. There is little for the officer to regulate on a truly private impoundment where fishing is concerned because licenses aren't required and nearly all harvest methods are legal. He might, however, find it necessary to check on bullfrog harvest from such ponds. On non-private ponds, the officer's responsibility increases. Here he may check for compliance with all the regulations that apply to fishing and frogging.

Both of our ponds are strictly private — for both construction and stocking no funds other than our own were used. The tributary of Pecan Creek that feeds our pond goes dry in summer and contains no fish.

Chapter 3

THE JOY OF A
BACKYARD LILY POOL

IN THIS CHAPTER we'll focus on a smaller and eminently doable kind of pond: the backyard lily pool. Regulations vary here, depending on the size pond and your water source. Check with your local authorities to learn what regulations exist.

We dug our own lily pond. Digging the hard Oklahoma clay in a dry summer wasn't easy, but we persisted, and by fall we'd hollowed out a rectangle 10 feet long by 5 feet wide by 3 feet deep. We built a wooden frame for the concrete, poured it, and stocked our pool with lilies and ornamental fish.

I must admit that my husband did most of the digging and concrete mixing; my contribution was minimal, but I was there with lots of moral support. I had the happy task of choosing the water lilies we would plant, along with the poolside shrubbery and flowers.

Creating the Pool

There are many ways of making a lily pool without going to as much trouble as we did. You can sink a wooden tub, discarded bathtub, or, in fact, any container of wood, porcelain, metal, plastic, or treated canvas that is 1 to 2 feet deep. They'll all work as well as a concrete-construction-type pool (like ours), in even the smallest garden. Metal garden pools are ideal for a secluded corner in an average-sized yard or worked into a plan for a penthouse garden.

You can also buy pre-formed ponds (see *Sources)*. They come in various graceful shapes and sizes, along with instructions for their installation. They are also more expensive than building your own.

Water Sources

Back to our lily pond. A year before we dug our ornamental pool, we put in a well. At that time we practiced water rationing almost every summer when rainfall became scanty and we wanted to have water for our garden. In later years, with Lake of the Arbuckles, Lake Murray, Lake Texoma, and numerous smaller lakes, our area became "water-rich," and water supplies were ample. But before that, water was scarce and very precious. Again we dug our own well, just like the biblical characters are described as doing — but we were more fortunate in having better equipment and supplies. My husband made a wooden frame for pouring the concrete, and our hard clay soil served us well. We had no cave-ins.

When we got down to about 20 feet, a funny incident occurred. (This is Oklahoma, and you can expect the unexpected.) We struck a gas pocket and it scared the bejabbies out

Water lily

of us. We almost knocked each other down scrambling to get up the ladder. We waited a while and nothing happened, so we went back to our work.

We struck water at about 25 feet. As it began seeping in we decided to go no deeper; we finished the well and set the pump. This was, of course, "surface water," not desirable for drinking but perfectly good for watering the garden or filling the lily/goldfish pond.

If you have no well, an underground line could be run from an outside faucet, with the water controlled through a valve hidden near the pond.

Using Concrete

We chose to construct our pond of concrete. While the labor was somewhat strenuous, the pliable nature of concrete allows molding into any shape you want to create. My husband, who was a graduate of New York State Agricultural College, had a good basic knowledge of plumbing, electrical wiring, and mixing concrete. If you have no previous experience with handling concrete, study a do-it-yourself book or watch a professional mix his in a wheelbarrow. Then observe how he pours it over his reinforcing rod or wire and then tamps it down.

Hog wire is good for reinforcing water features built from concrete. The wire should be held away from the bottom and sides of the feature so that the concrete will catch from above and below: Bricks or stones between the excavation and the wire will serve the purpose.

Fortunately, ready-mixed concrete can be purchased by the bag, so all that needs to be done is to add water for the right consistency. The key here is *stiff* but *pliable*.

When you pour concrete, you must start and finish the operation without any lag in time; otherwise, the concrete may leak when set up. Once poured, keep it moist for several days while it is curing.

Concrete will continue to harden throughout its lifetime, so fill the pond as soon as it feels solid to the touch. The pond must be filled and emptied three or four times at intervals of several days. This will get rid of the lime that dissolves from the concrete, which is harmful to fish and water plants.

Springs, Streams, and Waterfalls

If a waterfall or spring and a small stream are included in your plan, the stream bed must be poured at the same time as the pond. Some points to attend to when you pour these additions:

A pond/rill/spring combination requires flexible PVC tubing (I.D. ¾-inch is suggested) attached at the pond end to a submersible pump. Water is pumped uphill to the location of the waterfall or spring. Hide the tubing's upper end for a natural look.

The flow of the water must be deposited in a catch basin before it moves down the rill to the lower pond. The rill should be a meandering stream that will slow the water down and look more natural than if the water were to shoot in a straight line toward the pond.

Dig the stream bed deep enough to bury the flexible plastic water pipe beneath the concrete work and install the pipe before you pour. The concrete need be only 2 to 3 inches thick, but it too must be reinforced. Here you can use chicken wire.

Dig a trench 12 inches deep and 12 inches wide on both sides of the watercourse and fill it with pea gravel and sand. The trenches will take up any overflow during heavy rains and will also provide a foothold for ferns, crested iris, and other moisture-loving plants, including carnivorous plants and short-lived but colorful fungi on decaying wood.

Pumps

There are many submersible pumps on the market — we bought ours at a hardware store and it was relatively inexpensive — but take care in making your selection. If the pump does not match the height of the fall you need, it will soon wear out. One that is too large will be a better buy than one that is too small.

A pump that can handle 1,380 gallons of water per hour at 1 foot of elevation is just about right for operating a pond/rill/spring combination. With a 6-amp motor, it can lift 5 gallons of water a minute to a height of 20 feet.

Installation of this feature can be easy. Before installing the ¾-inch I.D. black tubing under the rill, adapt the end at the lower pond to standard male garden hose threads, and add a short length of flexible garden hose between the tubing and the pump (which also takes standard garden hose threads). It is then simple to connect the system by laying the pump on its side above a flat rock.

A word of caution: The electrical wiring required for the pump can be hazardous in combination with water if not handled properly. If you do the wiring yourself, be sure it is in accordance with electrical codes. If you lack experience in this type of work, have it done professionally.

It is best to put the wiring for the pump on a separate circuit to avoid overload. Always use special underground wiring and weatherproof receptacles in your garden area for safety as well as for appearance. The outlet for the pump should be close enough to the edge of the water feature that the pump cord (available in lengths to 25 feet) can be used without an extension cord.

If the service panel for the house wiring has unused space for circuit breakers, install a 20-amp breaker for the pump circuit. If the water feature is remote from the house, use 8- or 10-gauge wire with ground; otherwise, 12-gauge may be used.

The pump circuit must be placed in a trench at a depth where it can't be damaged by digging and planting. Be sure to mark its course so you won't forget where it is.

Ornamental Fish

You will want some ornamental fish, of course, and the choices are now so wide that it will be difficult for you not to get carried away and overbuy. So it is well to remember that the general rule of thumb is 1 inch of fish per 3 gallons of water. Recirculating the water by use of a fountain or waterfall will help increase your pond's oxygen content, as does plant life in the pond.

Check the pH level. A pH between 6.7 and 7.3 is ideal. This is extremely important in newly concreted ponds, as the concrete can turn the water very alkaline.

Take care not to overfeed your fish. Give new fish 48 hours to adjust to your pond before feeding them. Excessive feeding may cloud the

A backyard waterfall. *A rill of water meanders about 20 feet downslope from the catch basin, over a small ledge, and into a lower pond. Occasional overflow provides a boggy area for water-loving plants. The rill is about a foot wide. The lower pond is about 14 to 16 inches deep, 5 to 10 feet in diameter, with a surrounding border of rocks. Here's how to create it: Dig the stream bed. Install pipe, then pour concrete, reinforcing it with chicken wire. Dig a trench 12" deep and 12" wide on each side of the stream. Fill the trench with pea gravel and sand to catch the overflow. Place stones naturally and interplant them with ferns and iris.*

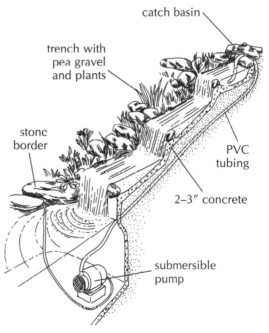

catch basin

trench with
pea gravel
and plants

stone
border

PVC
tubing

2–3" concrete

submersible
pump

water, as will feeding your fish bread and crackers. It is recommended that you use only the high-quality foods formulated for the type of fish you have chosen for your pond. *Discontinue feeding your fish whenever water temperature is below 45°F.*

Time to Plant

Stocking your pool is simple. Here's how: Tropicals and tender water lilies are favorites of pool gardeners. Day- or night-blooming varieties are prolific growers with showy, fragrant flowers often the size of dinner plates. Tropicals bear their flowers above water level on stems 6 to 18

Waterscaping

With the skeleton of the water feature completed, the fun part of dressing it up comes into focus. Here again, advance planning will help. What we are working toward is a natural look, and this can best be achieved with rocks of different sizes and shapes, placed as they would occur naturally. This will convert your pond into a rocky basin (assuming that you built your pond's sides sloping up and out from the bottom). Flat rocks look attractive tiered, all with the grain running horizontally, on top of one another and outward to the top of the pond.

You can then ring the edge with other rocks of various shapes. Hunting for just the right stones can be a fun family project all by itself. Take the kids along and let them gather, too — many years later they may come home and look to see if "their" rock is still in place! If possible, find native rocks that are well weathered and encrusted with moss and lichens. If not, the moss and lichens will grow there in their own good time (usually in just a few seasons). If the rocks are stacked loosely without mortar, there will be many pockets in which earth for growing plants can be placed; given long enough, it will accumulate naturally.

inches long. Colors range from white through the spectrum and include new species with blue-tipped chartreuse petals. Treat tropicals as annuals and purchase as growing plants at spring-planting time.

Water temperature should be 65°F or higher at the time of planting. Use large containers (at least 12 inches in diameter and 6 inches or more deep) for potting. Fill the container to within 2 inches of the top and plant the lily upright in the container center with its roots buried. Press soil firmly around buried portions, making sure the soil line is directly below the crown. Follow directions for fertilizing and add 1 inch of sand or gravel over the soil to hold it in place. Carefully lower the container into the pool, leaving 3 to 5 inches of water above the top of the container. Use bricks to bring the container up to the proper depth.

Which Water Lily?

Tropical water lilies that bloom at night open at dusk and stay open until noon the next day. Attractive *Nymphaea* cultivars include 'Trudy Slocum', which has large white flowers and foliage with serrated edges. 'Maroon Beauty' has deep maroon blooms and copper-toned leaves. 'Red Flare' has dark red petals and red-tinged foliage. 'Red Cup' has blood-red flowers and maroon foliage.

'Texas Shell Pink' is a lovely night-bloomer with large, light pink flowers. 'Sioux' opens a buff yellow, deepening as it matures to a peach color. It is very free flowering, and suitable for medium to large ponds. 'Graziella' (dwarf), with orange-red flowers and variegated leaves, is suitable for small ponds or tub gardens. 'Paul Hariott' has nicely mottled foliage and is excellent for tubs or small ponds.

If yellow is your favorite color, you'll have some lovely choices. Chromatella (*Nymphaea* 'Golden Cup') has yellow cup-shaped flowers with mottled leaves. A profuse bloomer, it is suitable for any sized pond.

'Texas Dawn' has the largest flowers, standing well above the water, and is a free bloomer. *N. Mexicana* is the smallest of all lilies. It has a striking yellow flower — nice for tub gardens. 'Helvola' is a tiny hardy lily (*N. tetragona*) ideal for tub gardens.

Night-blooming water lilies are the ultimate in summer romance. As the sun sets, the other water lilies fall asleep, but as the moon appears these fragrant, exotic flowers begin to unfold and they won't close until midmorning. To do best they require at least three but prefer six or more hours of direct sunlight. They like still water. They grow in Zones 3 to 11 during the summer and are frost tender. Tender perennials in Zone 9, they can survive winter in Zones 10 and 11. Night-blooming water lilies set the stage for evening entertainment. A poolside party or barbecue with friends can be great fun, and different.

You might not think that water lilies have predators, but they do. It is well to know about and watch out for them: muskrats, nutria, crawfish, ducks, geese, swan, deer, cattle, fish over 8 inches long, and turtles.

Named day-bloomers come in a variety of colors: 'Yellow Dazzler' with double blossoms; white 'Alice Tricker' with elongated petals and bright green leaves. These will grow in semishade. Sunset 'Albert Greenburg' comes in autumn shades and is noted for profuse blooming. 'Pink Star' has pink blossoms touched with lavender. Pink 'Louis Villemariette' flowers freely with large blossoms. Deep violet 'Director Moore' has a gold center with purple stamens. And, believe it or not, there is even a green — 'Green Smoke', a prolific grower with unusually colored flowers.

Hardy Water Lilies

Hardy water lilies are just as dazzling as the tropicals. They, too, come in an infinite variety and a myriad of colors. If you fancy white, there is 'Mount Shasta' or 'Perry's Double White' among the new introductions at Lilypons Water Gardens. Fragrant 'Marliacea Carnea' is a vigorous grower in pools 10 inches to 3 feet deep. It is a very light pink and makes a good cut flower. 'Mayla' is a fabulous fuchsia whose rich color makes it a show-stopper. 'Arc en Ciel', whose name means "Rainbow" in French, has magnificent variegated foliage of purple, rose, ivory, and bronze, framing a delicate pink flower. The list goes on and on, including 'Charlie Strawn', a good beginner's choice, and many delightful yellows and spectacular reds. 'James Brydon', a profuse-blooming red, is just as at home in a kettle garden as it is in a large pool.

Provide your water lilies with plenty of good, rich soil. A mixture of three parts topsoil to one part well-rotted manure will provide nutrients, or you may use three parts damp woodland or swamp soil and one part rotted manure. Use commercial dried manures if farmyard manure is not available. When planting in boxes, simply place the manure on the bottom and cover with topsoil. For a soil-bottomed pool, apply at least an 8-inch layer of this mixture. When planting tropical varieties, increase to a 12-inch layer. Peat moss and sand should *not* be mixed with the soil.

Hardy water lilies grow horizontally. Use large containers (at least 12 inches in diameter and 6 inches or more deep) for potting and fill with soil to within 2 inches of the top of the container. Fertilize. (There are tablets for this, sold by companies specializing in water lilies. See *Sources.*) Plant the hardy tuber at a 45-degree angle with the crown protruding above the soil line. Add 1 inch of sand or gravel over the top of the soil. Carefully lower the container into the pool, leaving 6 to 8 inches of water above the top of the container. Use bricks or concrete blocks to adjust planting depth.

Lotus

Lotus *(Nelumbo)* tubers are fragile and need extreme care in handling. The tuber consists of an elongated fleshy body that resembles a banana. It will have a growing point and one or more joints. Use a large container (15 inches or more in diameter). Fill with rich soil to within 2 inches of the container rim. Fertilize following directions. Scoop a slight depression in the soil, place the tuber in the depression, and cover with 2 inches of soil. Cover the soil with 1 inch of gravel, avoiding the tender growing points. Lower in pool leaving 3 to 4 inches of water above the growing tips.

Iris for the Poolside

Having paid proper court to the more dramatic inhabitants, we must not forget the many varieties of iris that grow poolside or even in the water at the edge of the pond. These come in a variety of colors —

Freshening Your Pond

On occasion, you may want to freshen the pond, as heavy rains sometimes discolor the water. Use a submersible pump to draw down the lower pond completely, but leave enough water in the bottom for the fish to remain comfortable. Or transfer them to a holding tank until the pond fills.

Winter care depends on where you live. In a warm, southern climate you may need to do nothing. In a more severe climate it would probably be wise to drain the pond or winterize it with boards and bales of hay or straw.

During winter, keep as many leaves as possible out of your pond. This can be done by putting a nylon mesh over the pond or by netting them out. Decaying leaves release noxious gases that may be harmful to your fish. In our area, we keep an open spot in the ice by placing an automatic heater in the pond. This enables gases to escape from the pond. In a colder part of the country, where temperatures stay below zero for weeks at a time, this would not work, because the pond would freeze solid and ruin both net and heater. Wherever you live, *do not crack or break ice. The shock waves can give your fish a fatal concussion.*

Delmar J. Robinson, writing in *Troy-Bilt Owner News,* advises taking up the pump every winter, cleaning it, and knocking off what little rust there is on the metal screws. Then spray the housing with a very light coating of WD-40 and put the pump in storage.

If there is a chance your pond will freeze hard, it is best to set pots of hardy lilies in the deepest part, or store them over winter in a cool, moist place. Treat tropical lilies as annuals — and choose some new lovelies next spring.

white, yellow, blue, red, and deep purple — and a variety also of shapes and sizes. There is 'Black Gamecock', with rich blue-black flowers (a Louisiana hybrid). Another Louisiana hybrid, 'Eolian', has large, magnificent, sky blue flowers. 'Kirk Strawn' is an incredible vermilion, and 'Red Iris', a Native American plant, has thin, narrow leaves that give it a graceful appearance and complement the rosy red bloom.

Marginal Plants

These are the shallow water plants that provide the transition from water to land. And they are available in both hardy and tropical varieties. If you fancy the tropicals, you can take some from the pool and winter them over as houseplants. Marginal plants look best when used in masses, just as you would find them in nature. But use them with caution, for they are rampant growers and, if planted in earth-bottom ponds, will take over. Lilypons recommends that iris and sweet flag be used in earth-bottom ponds. These plants, and hardy water lilies, have the same predators as those listed for tropical water lilies.

Ruby-eye arrowhead (*Sagittaria montevidensis*) has dazzling purple eyes that smile through white petals and its leaves are deep green and lush. It grows to 30 inches tall, will thrive in full sun to shade, and is winter hardy in Zones 9 to 11.

Curly mint is a plant of lush-creeping growth and delightful fragrance. It grows to 6 inches and thrives in full sun to shade. Ribbon grass (*Phalaris arundiinacea*), a brilliant pond accent for fall, has been playfully named 'Strawberries and Cream'. The graceful 24-inch leaves, striped white in spring and summer, greet the fall in shades of pink.

Plants for a Shady Location

If your pond is in a woodland area where a moderate amount of moisture can be depended on during the growing season, there are many ferns and wildflowers that can be used at little cost, beginning with the native plants that thrive in your area. The evaporation and misting of moving water in the garden will help provide this mini-rainforest habitat with moisture. The ferns that exult in a moist area make an impressive list. Resurrection ferns *(Polypodium polypodioides)* turn brown when dry but, true to their name, revive when they become wet. This small fern and the common polypody *(Polypodium virginianum)* grow on rocks, logs, and trees.

Camptosorus rhizophyllus, the walking fern, has long, narrow leaves. New plants grow where the tips of the leaves touch the soil; hence the name "walking." They grow on limestone rock and in limestone soil.

One of the more beautiful ferns, maidenhair *(Adiantum pedatum)* thrives when its roots are wedged into openings among rocks, filled with rich humus.

Ferns at the boggy or swampy end of a combination water feature make lovely group plantings. The most widely used are lady fern *(Athyrium Filix-femina),* royal fern *(Osmunda regalis),* and cinnamon fern *(Osmunda cinnamomea).* Wayside Gardens has a nice selection of hardy ferns (see *Sources*). Try to choose ferns native to your area.

For a realistic, natural look, mosses and lichens are an important part of a water feature. Hunt around (make this another family outing) and look for rocks on which they are already growing. Even if they look dry, they will revive and multiply in a moist pond area.

Native Wildflowers and Shrubs

Plan for an assortment of native wildflowers. Applewood Seed Company has seeds for every region of the country. If you live in the southwest, Plants of the Southwest has native plants that will grow for you.

Native shrubs that do well in shady water gardens are *Euonymus americanus* (strawberry bush, or hearts a-burstin'), *Itea virginica* (sweet spires), and *Lindera benzoin* (spicebush). All are to some degree fragrant and will also act as taller foils for plants of lesser stature.

Apart from already existing canopy trees, you may want to plant some "understudy" trees — seedlings 3 to 4 feet tall or more. A good choice would be sweet gums, with their star-shaped leaves, or sassafras (the mitten tree), with variable-shaped, light green foliage. These trees also add glorious fall color to the landscape.

Low-growing ground covers can also help to make the area more attractive. Lily of the valley is fragrant and can grow in partial shade. *Vinca minor,* with its pretty blue flowers, is a lovely plant and a rampant grower, which works well if you have large spaces to cover. *Ajuga reptans* is a bronze-leafed creeper with rich purple flowers. Plumbago does well in sun or shade and thrives in any soil, producing sky blue flowers from July to frost. Hardy verbena makes an easy-care, no-mow carpet and is loaded with reddish purple flowers.

In a cool, moist climate you might want to round out the dressing of your water feature with fungi. Rotting wood and old stumps go well with a water scene, suggesting your pond has met fairy approval. Many fungi have beautiful coloration, and striated mushrooms are fascinating additions during their own short season.

Sharing Water with Wildlife

If wildlife has priority in your water garden plan, it's a good idea to follow a few guidelines. Patio Garden Ponds (see *Sources*) suggests that the slopes of the pool's sides be constructed with an area of shallow "beach," so that creatures can climb into and out of the pool easily. Place an assortment of flat-bottomed stones near the water's edge to provide refuge for a variety of animal life. You can create a boggy area, vital to many amphibians and birds, by forming a ridge in the contour of the pool between the deeper zone of water in the center and a shallow area near the side, and filling with soil. This will accommodate plants, which can then intermingle freely. Use native plants wherever possible, as these are known to attract wildlife more readily.

What Do You Want to Attract?

What you plant to some extent determines the woodland visitors who will come to your poolside. The National Wildlife Federation believes that in ideal wildlife management, the plan should supply as much food as possible through vegetation, in order to meet the year-round needs of many species. Shrubs, trees, and other plants that produce acorns and nuts, berries, buds, catkins, fruit, nectar, and seeds should be included wherever possible.

Plant trees or shrubs that will provide food for wildlife all year long. In the Northeast, for example, mountain ash bears fruit from August to March. Contact a local nature, nursery, or garden center to find out the best food plants for your area.

Plants of the Southwest (see *Sources*) recommends natural wild bird-seed for the Southwest that will grow in many other parts of the country. Among the seed eaters are nuthatches, titmice, sparrows, finches, siskins, towhees, juncos, jays, Clark's nutcracker, and, of course, quail, pheasant, and doves.

Many native trees, shrubs, perennials, and annuals will attract seed-eating birds. Consider spruce, fir, birch, pine, oak, and paloverde. Coreopsis, cosmos, sunflowers, verbesina, and thistles are excellent smaller flowering plants. Burnet and croton are favorites of doves. Many native grasses have seeds relished by birds — bluegrasses (*Poa* species), grama grasses *(Bouteloua),* bluestems *(Andropogon* species), wheat grasses *(Agropyron* species), and Indian rice grass *(Oryzopsis hymenoides)* are all excellent choices. You can plant them for lawns and wildflower meadows as well.

Birds need nesting sites too, and shelter from the weather and predators. Acorns and browse are all provided by native oaks, which are veritable delicatessens for wildlife. Strong limbed, deep rooted, drought

Frogs and Turtles

"Build it and they will come" is a sadly overworked phrase but it can certainly be applied to frogs and turtles — if there is water anywhere about, they will find it, as will most of the forest creatures, including rabbits and deer.

tolerant, and handsome, oaks vary in habit from low shrubs to commanding trees and may be evergreen or deciduous.

Many of the same shrubs, trees, and seed plants that attract birds will also attract squirrels and chipmunks, in some cases providing them nesting places as well.

Hummingbird Flowers

Because many people find hummingbirds special, I'm going to touch on their favorite food plants so you can enjoy them, too, by attracting them to your garden. Fifteen different species of tiny iridescent hummingbirds flash through western gardens. The one to look for in the East is the widespread rubythroat. Like most birds, hummers have excellent

Just for Fun: Let's Consider Snails

In about 48 B.C., a Roman gourmet named Fulvius Hilpinus actually had enclosures constructed in his garden in which snails could breed and feed. Their food was a special mixture of sweet wine, honey, and flour. The Romans loved to eat snails, which they believed could ease labor pains, cure hangovers, and act as a love potion.

Snails are easy enough to catch — the proverbial snail's pace is only about one mile in three weeks — but care should be taken to gather only edible species. All snails can be fatally poisonous. Because they love to eat deadly nightshade, henbane, and wartwort, they must be starved for two weeks or so after capture to clear their digestive systems and then fattened on a special diet, much as the Romans did. Cook them by soaking live snails in salt water for three hours, washing them, and plunging them into boiling water for 30 minutes.

To eat snails, hold the shell in one hand, withdraw the tasty meat with a two-pronged snail fork, and dip the snail in a garlicky butter sauce. Serve snails with a white wine if they are to be an appetizer, and a red wine if they will be the main course.

vision and are attracted to bright red flowers, which they home in on from great distances. But once in your garden they will visit flowers of any color in search of nectar and small insects.

The flowers that attract them are long and tubular, often borne sideways or drooping, and contain copious nectar. Hummingbirds hover before the flowers, and insert their long bills and tongues for the nectar, all the while whirring their wings — more than 3,000 times a minute!

The ruby-throated hummingbird, a tropical jewel, is lured to the north by flowers it finds desirable, such as the wild columbine's five inverted horns of plenty, the monarda or bee balm, the coral honeysuckle, and other flowers wearing its favorite color. In the Southwest the birds are drawn by red columbine *(Aquilegia elegantula)* and Indian paintbrush *(Castilleja integra)*. In spring, plant scarlet bugler *(Penstemon*

A Movable Pool

Some people will go to almost any length to have a water garden. I once had a creative neighbor whose husband's job required them to move frequently. I went to visit her one summer afternoon and found her sitting in her lawn chair in the shade by her tiny "pool." It was so cleverly designed and disguised that I did not immediately realize that it was simply the lid of a metal trash can. The bottom had a light covering of white sand, with a few small, rosy pink shells. A "landing stone" graced the center. Rocks and small plants were arranged around the edge, artfully concealing the rim. Even as we chatted, a black swallowtail butterfly swooped down gracefully, perched on the landing stone, and unfurled its long tongue, quite unabashed by our presence.

As we quietly watched, she told me she had a "traveling kit" for her arrangement and took the components with her when they moved. Having her small quiet pool, she said, gave her a feeling of inner tranquility as nothing else did to help her adjust to their constantly changing environment. "And," she added, smiling, "some day, when we settle down, I'm going to have a *real* pool with fish and lots of water lilies — like yours."

barbatus) and skyrocket *(Ipomopsis aggregata)*, and in
the summer hummingbird trumpet
(Zauschneria latifolia), which also
grows well into the fall. Some
species, such as Indian paintbrush, scarlet hedge-nettle
(Stachys coccinea), and autumn sage *(Salvia greggii)*, begin
blooming in early spring and are
stopped only by fall frosts.

In addition to the flowers in
nature's garden, many that have been
brought from the ends of the earth to
grace our garden plots please the hum-
mer no less. Canna, nasturtium, phlox,
trumpet flower, salvia, and a host of others delight its eye and its palate
as well. The birds migrate in May and October.

Butterfly Attractions

The "flying flowers" are everywhere, even coming to a penthouse
garden when flowers to their liking are planted there. Many butterflies see
red, and butterfly flowers are often brilliantly colored — deep pink, scarlet, bright blue — and generally very fragrant. Butterfly weed *(Asclepias
tuberosa)* is a spectacular vivid orange. Its cousin, the common milkweed
(Asclepias speciosa), has silvery pink flowers and is the specific host plant
of the regal monarch butterfly. Some other excellent butterfly plants are
indigo bush *(Amorpha fruticosa* and *A. canescens)*, dogbane *(Apocynum
androsaemifolium)*, shrubby cinquefoil *(Potentilla fruticosa)*, and cutleaf
coneflower *(Rudbeckia laciniata)*.

Chapter 4

POND PLANTS

MANY DIFFERENT AQUATIC PLANTS can be found in, on, and around ponds, ranging from microscopic organisms known as plankton algae, which drift suspended in the water, to large plants rooted in the pond bottom. Some aquatic plants are beautiful, fragrant, interesting, even edible; some are desirable as food for fish or waterfowl; some are considered weeds that might choke your pond. Wind, birds, aquatic animals, and even people scatter seeds.

Beneficial Plants: The Good Guys

Many water plants are of enormous value to fish and wildlife, providing food and shelter and stabilizing the aquatic environment. The great majority of water plants never cause trouble in ponds and lakes, including semiaquatic, shoreline, and moist-soil plants. *Water Plants for Missouri Ponds*, a book put out by the Missouri Department of Conservation, identifies these in four habitat sections — shoreline, emergent, floating, and submerged.

44

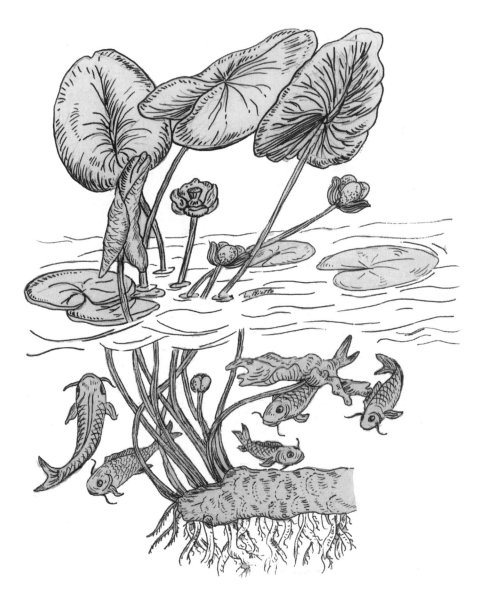

Spatterdock, an emergent plant, provides valuable shade and shelter at the pond's edge.

Shoreline Plants

Wild **iris** are some of our most lovely shoreline plants, growing best in rich, moist, acid soil. They are ideal plants for the pond edge. They never cause any problems, and have lovely flowers in the spring. Each flower has three petals and three larger, petal-like sepals, forming the classic fleur-de-lis shape. Leaves are slender and blade-like, and the plants spread slowly from shallow, creeping rootstocks. The two most suited to the water's edge are the southern blue flag *(Iris virginica)* and **copper iris** *(Iris fulva)*. Rhizomes of blue flag have long been used medicinally. Yellow iris *(Iris pseudacorus)* is another suggestion; it is a Japanese iris type.

Calamus or **sweet flag** *(Acorus calamus)* is an attractive, interesting, nonaggressive pondside plant, low enough to be fished over yet growing in clumps that provide nesting spots for fish. Calamus has long enjoyed the reputation of being a "living drugstore": It was used to treat many ills in days gone by when apothecaries were few and far between. The root was chewed raw or prepared as a tea or salve, either alone or mixed with other plants. It has been used as a stimulant, insulin substitute, and even as a cough medicine. Since the time of Hippocrates (circa 400 B.C.) it has enjoyed a reputation as a healing herb, treating such health problems as fever, indigestion, toothache, burns, colic, tuberculosis, and eye diseases. In pioneer America it was often strewn over clay floors to provide a pleasant aroma when walked upon.

It is propagated by root division in the spring. Plant the rhizomes just a few inches below the soil in shallow water (1 to 9 inches deep). Calamus competes well with cattails and may be planted in areas where cattails are not desirable. A lovely variegated type is now available (see *Sources*).

Iris

Rose mallow *(Hibiscus lasiocarpos).* A very desirable pond plant, rose mallow is exceptionally beautiful when planted at the pond's edge. It grows quite tall, however, and should not be planted on a bank used for fishing. Enjoy just a few rose mallows, limiting them to two or three plants to keep the shoreline open. You can easily control the spread by picking off the seed capsules in the fall. Hibiscus (an old Roman name for rose mallow) prefers moist soil or shallow water, though it can grow in drier areas. The five white petals are rolled in the bud, and spiral open to reveal a deep purple center. Most of the plant is covered with velvety hair, including the stem, seed capsules, and both sides of the leaf. Game birds such as ducks and quail eat the seeds, and it is considered a good plant for wildlife refuges. Roots are demulcent and emollient, good in cough remedies.

Horsetails *(Equisetum* spp.). Looking as if they belong in a prehistoric landscape along with dinosaurs and giant dragonflies, they are indeed the direct descendants of the enormous horsetails that grew more than 50 feet tall in the primeval forests of the Coal Age, 300 million years ago. Their dark green, segmented tubes can be easily popped apart at the joints (granddaughter Laura Elizabeth discovered this when she was small). They are covered with a layer of silica crystals, which give them a sandpapery feel. They possess no true leaves, but the primitive beginnings of leaves appear as scaly sheaths at the joints. The stems may be simple or have whorls of branches. Decorative and interesting plants for the pond's edge, they bind the soil, can be fished over, and do not invade water more than a few inches deep. Even so, they can become a problem in low-lying areas of crop fields, spreading rapidly. They have deep roots, so they are difficult to eradicate once established. If you fancy them, they grow well in containers, creating an attractive vertical accent. German housewives once used the fibers for scrubbing pots and pans.

Burhead *(Echinodorus berteroi).* This is an attractive plant for fishing ponds, as it grows singly in shallow water close to shore and rarely becomes a problem. Burhead looks much like its close relative **water plantain** *(Alisma triviale),* also a desirable pond plant. Both have whorls of long-stemmed leaves with parallel veins, and tall, branched flower stalks. But the flower stalks of water plantain are more delicate and feathery and the seed heads are not spiny. Burhead has many small, white flowers, each with three petals. Its base is bulblike and fleshy. Propagate burhead by seeds or from cuttings of the rootstock. If the plant receives more than 12 hours of daily illumination, it is likely to develop floating and emergent leaves. It will flower from July through September.

Species of *Echinodorus* are used for medicinal purposes in South America and the West Indies. Teas, root extracts, and other preparations have been used as tonics, diuretics, laxatives, and gargles, as well as to clean and heal the skin.

Water pepper (*Polygonum hydropiperoides*). A member of the smartweed family, this is a pond desirable because it stays at the shoreline and will not grow in deep water. It has attractive flowers that bloom all summer and fall. The seeds are excellent food for waterfowl and songbirds.

Mud plantain (*Heteranthera reniformis*). This is a harmless, attractive plant for the pond shoreline or shallow water. Growing readily, it will not crowd out other aquatic plants. It may be propagated from slips, which readily root at the nodes. Its dainty white or pale blue flowers are clustered on a spike.

Water parsnip (*Sium suave*). A striking accent for the pond's edge, water parsnip is welcome because it is not a rampant grower. Flowering is from July through September. The roots of water parsnip are edible when prepared as a cooked vegetable. However, the plant is very similar to water hemlock, which you must never use as a food plant. Water hemlock is violently poisonous and has been responsible for many cattle poisonings and a number of human deaths.

Other shoreline plants you might consider include **lizard's tail** (*Saururus cernuus*), which has unusual flowers and a pleasant odor. The plants produce a thick mat of rhizomes, which are helpful in stabilizing pond shorelines. It grows to 24 inches high.

We planted *Proso millet*, or **duck millet.** It grows fast, producing abundant seed for waterfowl, and has good drought resistance.

Emergent Plants

Emergent plants are those that root in water but have stems and leaves standing above water.

Pickerelweed *(Pontederia cordata)* adds color and interest to the edge of the pond. One of our most beautiful plants, it has some other good qualities: It grows slowly, remains in shallow water, and does not become rampant. The lovely, showy blue flowers are a delight all summer long. Since almost no other water plants have flowers of the violet-blue of pickerelweed, it is easy to identify, standing out vividly at the water's edge.

Pickerelweed may be transplanted or grown from roots. If you locate a large stand, ask permission of the owner to collect a limited amount. It may also be propagated by seed. The leaves are decorative, too, of a vivid glassy green and lance- or heart-shaped, growing in a rosette from a thick rootstock. The distinctive seed of the spike blooms has prominent toothed ridges. Dried and ground, the fruits with their starchy seeds make acceptable flour substitutes.

Spatterdock *(Nuphar lutea)* is of value at the pond's edge because its large, attractive leaves shade out less desirable plants. It provides shelter for fish and animals and grows slowly, staying in shallower water. It is recommended to improve the habitat of fishing ponds and lakes. Also known as **cowlily**, spatterdock grows in water from 6 inches to 2 feet.

The spatterdock blossom behaves rather strangely. It opens just slightly and then closes at night for four or five days. On the first day we are charmed by its intensely sweet smell, something like papaya fruit or brandy. But on the second day the scent changes to a less pleasant, fermented odor that, fortunately, is not as strong. Spatterdock has its own special pollinators, the long-horned leaf beetles *(Donacia piscatrix),* which may be trapped in the flowers when the petals close. The beetles operate at night and by morning they are covered with pollen, which they carry to other blossoms.

Spike rushes *(Eleocharis* spp.) are slender, grasslike plants, desirable to establish on the pond bottom where they create a lovely green underwater "lawn," helpful in keeping aquatic weeds from taking hold. Spike rushes come in various sizes. The taller **square-stem spike rush** is very attractive in bloom, and forms a good cover for erosion control along banks and dams and in moist, inlet areas. Spike rushes are good for fishing ponds as they do not interfere with casting and never overrun the pool. They grow in tufts along thin, trailing underground roots. Plant from April to August. These inoffensive little plants bind the shoreline soil and provide shelter for fish, amphibians, and insects, and are a good wildlife food source.

Thalia *(Thalia dealbata)* is another showy, beautiful plant for the pond's edge, growing slowly and easily controlled. This is a protected plant in some states and should be obtained from aquatic plant nurseries.

Thalia may stand up to 6 feet tall. Its huge, cannalike leaves sprout from a thick base, giving the plant a tropical appearance. Because the leaves are dusted with a fine white powder, it is sometimes called powdery thalia. Two or three plants of thalia would make a charming accent. Because it is not winter-hardy in the north, some pond owners prefer to grow thalia in pots, bringing it indoors in fall for winter protection. Propagate by root division in the spring and plant in rich compost in shallow water or wet soil. Another striking feature of thalia is its flower stalk — a long wand bearing clusters of purple blossoms. This showy plant is sometimes called **water canna**.

Thalia belongs to the large arrowroot family (Marantaceae) and is named for Johann Thal, a German naturalist of the sixteenth century. The name *dealbata* means "white-washed", and refers to the plant's powdery coating.

Arrowheads *(Sagittaria* spp.) are so named because of the "sagittate" or arrow-shaped leaf, the hallmark of this family, which makes them easy to identify. Sagittarias grow only along the water's edge, making them ideal plants for fishing ponds and lakes. Easy to grow yet nonaggressive, they have attractive leaves and flowers and are beneficial for wildlife. They are particularly good for shallow water and shoreline areas, helpful especially if erosion is a problem. The white flowers are much admired.

The "duck potato" *(S. latifolia)* is the most common arrowhead and the one from which duck potatoes are commonly gathered. Waterfowl eagerly search for the duck potatoes, and many kinds of water birds and songbirds also eat the seeds. This plant has been introduced to many wetland areas to improve feeding habitat for ducks and geese. Duck potatoes were also once an important food source for Native Americans. Members of the Lewis and Clark expedition ate them, as did many early settlers.

Arrowhead plants are easy to transplant and grow. They can be introduced around a pond by broadcasting the seed in fall or spring or by setting the tubers from March 1 to August 1. Space plants along the shoreline 3 feet apart, in water up to 1 foot deep. They need rich soil with plenty of light.

Broad-fruited bur reed (*Sparganium eurycarpum*) is welcome around fishing ponds as it is never a problem, provides both food and cover for waterfowl, and is attractive in either the grassy or underwater form. Small colonies of bur reeds are found along the edges of ponds, lakes, and rivers, growing in damp soil or shallow waters. They thrive in both temperate and cold regions. The seeds are eaten by waterfowl and marsh birds, and are a significant part of the diet of mallards and whistling swans. Stands of bur reed are also used for roosting and making nests. Deer eat the entire plant. The plant does not have burrs that adhere to animals or clothing.

Propagate by division, and set out the plants in shallow water. Bur reeds are not recommended for ornamental water gardens but are useful for pond borders and other wild settings.

Hedge hyssop (*Gratiola virginiana*) provides an attractive cover for a muddy area and inhibits less desirable plants. It will not spread into deep water or grow tall enough to interfere with fishing.

The 20 species of hedge hyssop are generally found in the wet areas of the Temperate Zone. They flower from April to October. Hedge hyssop is a rather coarse-looking plant. A relative of the snapdragon, its upper stem bears tubular blossoms that are white, tinged with pink or yellow. It has straight stems and serrated leaves, and often grows in colonies.

Multitudes of tiny seeds are produced by the round seed capsules. The seeds are dispersed by the wind, allowing the plant to colonize new ponds. Hedge hyssop is propagated either by the seeds or by root division.

The plant has been used medicinally for the treatment of dropsy, intermittent fever, worms, and bruises.

Cattails Are Not All Bad

Cattails (*Typhaceae*) in your catfish pond are not desirable, but sometimes they grow there anyway, and they're difficult to eradicate. So we might need to practice the old adage, "If you can't whip 'em, join 'em!"

These striking plants grow in a muck-type bottom and are seldom a good indicator of fish habitat except in early spring, when northern pike will use these weedy areas for spawning. Largemouth bass may use floating mats of cattails for cover.

According to Grace Firth, writing in *A Natural Year*, "Bulbous tubers from the shoots of cattail roots may be peeled and boiled in salted water for ten to twenty minutes, then served drenched in butter, salt and pepper. With crisp-fried fish they are delicious."

Ben Charles Harris, in *Eat the Weeds*, also has a lot to say about cattails. He notes uses for the root stalk, lower leaf stem, the young shoots, fruiting flowerheads (spikes), and the down.

The central portion of the root stalk is mainly starch. After it is collected and completely dried, it is easily ground into fine meal and used like arrowleaf. The early settlers of Virginia ate the cooked roots and were fond of them.

The inner portions of the root and stem are cut into 1- or 2-inch segments and cooked in soups or stews. Collect the young stems in spring. Cut them 10 to 12 inches from the root, peel off the outer rind, and add them to a vegetable salad.

When the first young shoots appear in spring, they are whitish and crisp, and may be used as an asparagus substitute. Serve them as a cooked vegetable; the mildly marshy odor is quickly dispelled by warm water.

A treat is in store for the enterprising cook who would like to make a bread from the pollen heads or down. You'll need about 20 to 25 good-sized pollen heads to yield a small loaf. It is best to mix an equal portion of pure whole-wheat flour so that uniformity and adhesiveness are more easily obtained. Cattail flour — especially of the pollen, it is reported — contains protein, sulphur, phosphorus, carbohydrates, sugar, and oil.

The narrow leaf cattail *(Typha augustifolia)* furnishes a very fine background in massed plantings for lily pools.

Soft rush (*Juncus effusus*) grows densely in very shallow water but never invades deeper areas. Thick stands are short enough to fish over and may be helpful in preventing the encroachment of cattails. Historically, it has been an economically valuable plant. Its long use for mats and seating continues in many areas throughout the world. *Juncus effusus* is not a native of North America but was introduced from Europe. It was important in medieval England, India, and China, where homes were commonly illuminated with "rushlights." These were lengths of peeled rush, soaked in wax or grease and lighted at one end like a candle. The pith of soft rush is absorbent, making the plant ideal for this purpose. Waterfowl, songbirds, and game birds like the seeds. The clumped stems provide spawning habitat for sunfish and other types of fish. And if little fish are to grow into big fish, they need protective areas to hide in so they will not be eaten.

River bulrush root (*Scirpus fluviatilis*) makes excellent cover and food for wildlife, as well as controlling erosion.

Bulrushes (*Scirpus* spp.). Mention bulrushes and I always think of the biblical story in which the princess-sister of the Pharaoh found Moses in the bulrushes in a reed basket, and adopted him. A lot of people are skeptical about this, believing he was her son and she hid him there. Perhaps. Ancient Egypt no doubt had its press agents who put out whatever the Pharaoh told them to.

Bulrushes vary in their suitability for fishing ponds; some types are beautiful and nonaggressive, others become pernicious weeds. Growing thickly, their value for soil-binding of wetlands is enormous. They also have almost as many edible parts as do cattails, and can be used in similar ways. The roots were eaten both raw and cooked by Native Americans, and the tribes of the Northwest crushed and boiled the young roots, which yield a sweet syrup. The pollen can be pressed into cakes and baked, and the ground-up seeds yield cereal or flour. Young winter shoots are tasty raw or cooked, as are the tender cores at the bases of the stems.

Consider these plants for erosion control. The reeds grow in shallow water, and when the bottom is hard, they can be a good indicator of a largemouth bass spawning area.

Propagate bulrushes by planting pieces of roots and shoots, or by seeds.

Floating Plants

The **fragrant water lily** *(Nymphaea odorata)* is a suitable candidate for medium to large ponds, requiring only a little effort to control its spread. It has been estimated that a planted tuber grows slowly, covering roughly a 15-foot-diameter circle in approximately five years. Even so, trimming back occasionally is advisable. Do this in spring by following new stems down to the root and breaking off the growing tips. Water lilies, planted in ponds, have the virtue of increasing wildlife food production and cover. Ponds containing bluegills and redear are especially benefited by this lovely pond plant. My son, on his fishing expeditions as a teenager, would occasionally bring me a blossom or two and I would float them in a large shallow bowl as a table centerpiece so we could enjoy their beauty and fragrance as long as possible.

Lilies can hold largemouth bass, when combined with other weed growth or easy access to deep water. The **white water lily** *(Nymphaea tuberosa)* gives beauty plus food and cover for game fish.

Leaves and flowers are attached to flexible underwater stalks, rising from the thick rhizomes. At the final closing of the flowers, the flower stalk corkscrews, drawing the developing fruit below the water. Growth from the rhizome and seeds are the means of reproduction. This plant is not difficult to grow. See Chapter 3, "The Joy of a Backyard Lily Pool," for more on water lilies.

American featherfoil *(Hottonia inflata)* is an unusual plant you might like to experiment with cautiously. Little is known about it, but featherfoil has a strange beauty all its own as it drifts about on the water's surface during spring and summer, buoyed up by a cluster of swollen, air-filled flowering stalks, each bearing a ring of tiny white blossoms. Occasionally, a number of plants drift free in large mats.

Frogbit *(Limnobium spongia),* found on the surface of quiet waters, is a small drifter sometimes called sponge plant. This is because of the floating leaves, which have air-filled tissue on their undersides. Its aerial leaves, heart-shaped (inspiring another common name — giant water violet), reach above the water on long stems. The small male flowers and the cream-colored female flowers with long fuzzy stigmas appear on separate plants. The numerous runners make propagation easy. Never known, so far, to become a problem, it may be useful in discouraging less desirable floating plants such as duckweeds.

Submerged Plants

Wild celery *(Vallisneria americana)*, beloved of ducks, is the best pond plant for fish. The leaves of wild celery, almost completely submerged, provide good fish habitat without running rampant or interfering with fishing. Growing thickly, it may even crowd out other, less desirable water plants. Waterfowl love it. Growing singly, wild celery looks like a bundle of long, green ribbons tied at one end with string and anchored at the pond bottom. Although these ribbons are paper-thin and less than ½-inch wide, they are fairly tough and may grow as long as 7 feet. The prominent stripe in each leaf distinguishes it from other underwater plants. Strangely, the male and female flowers of wild celery form underwater on different plants before rising to the surface. The pollination process takes place when hundreds of tiny male flower buds develop in a translucent envelope at the base of the plant. Over a period of several days, flower buds are released from the envelope. Each contains a tiny air bubble that carries it to the surface, where it opens, and the flower forms a small boat.

Water purslane *(Ludwigia palustris)*. Growing only in shallow water, purslane is attractive and valuable for the pond's edge, standing occasionally a few inches above the surface. It makes its appearance early in the spring, adding a distinctive touch of color underwater or along the pond edge. It is propagated by cuttings, needs good light, and grows best in a temperature of 55°–60°F. It sheds its lower leaves in autumn. Propagate from the stem tips in spring, or you can plant the seeds in shallow sand.

Water star grass *(Heteranthera dubia)* makes a nice cover plant for pond shorelines, and its dainty yellow flowers are a pleasing accent. As do many other water plants, it provides food for waterfowl and protection for small fish. Water star grass does well in full illumination and likes alkaline water. It will propagate readily from cuttings or divisions and tolerates a wide range of water temperature, depth, and flow.

Water starwort *(Callitriche heterophylla)* is a small, inoffensive aquatic plant that never becomes a problem and provides cover for fish and fish-food organisms. Waterfowl, especially ducks, eat the seeds and herbage. It requires shallow water, cool temperatures, and adequate light. Several cultivated varieties are available. *Callitriche,* the genus name, is derived from the Greek words *kalos,* meaning "beautiful," and *thrix,* meaning "hair," apparently referring to the attractive appearance of the plant.

Water starwort grows moderately, stays close to shore, appears early in spring, and dies back when warmer weather arrives.

Aquatic Weeds

Intensive fish production often involves adding large amounts of commercial feeds and inorganic fertilizers to ponds. Nutrients introduced into the water through feeds and fertilizers often create an ideal habitat for aquatic weed growth. Submersed aquatic weeds are particularly undesirable because fish-harvesting seines will ride up over the weeds and allow fish to escape. Ponds with dense weed infestations can be almost impossible to harvest since the weight of the weeds accumulating in the seine can become too great to be pulled. Additionally, separating fish from weeds is a slow process and can severely stress fish.

Aquatic plants that cause weed problems may be placed into five groups: shoreline weeds, algae, floating weeds, emersed weeds (foliage above water), and submersed weeds (majority of foliage below water).

Algae

Algae are the most common group of weeds in aquaculture ponds. Shape and size vary from microscopic single- or multiple-celled plants to branched plants that resemble submersed aquatic weeds. Unlike other aquatic plants, algae do not produce flowers or seeds. Algae are divided into three groups: plankton algae, filamentous algae (pond moss), and the stoneworts (*Chara* spp. and *Nitella* spp.).

Sand grass (*Chara* and *Nitella*) is a ragged, matted algae that seldom grows more than a foot high off the bottom and gives off a musky odor when crushed between the fingers. It is completely submerged. In northern states it can be a prime indicator of largemouth spawning habitat.

Plankton algae produce most of the dissolved oxygen in a pond and are essential to fish survival. In the presence of sunlight, green plants release oxygen as a by-product of photosynthesis. At night, plants and other pond organisms consume oxygen. Because of this diurnal cycle, oxygen concentrations are lowest at dawn and highest in mid-afternoon. Cycle imbalances can lead to oxygen depletion and eventually fish death.

In commercial fish ponds, excessive plankton algae may result from the high feeding rates necessary to produce large fish yields. In many cases, fish production rates are limited by the amount of feed that can be applied without plankton algae blooms becoming so dense that dissolved oxygen problems cannot be managed. The complexity of this cycle makes attempts to treat ponds with algicides to "thin out" excess algae growth very risky. Although spot treatments of plankton algae scums are effective, problems with low dissolved oxygen concentrations following algicide applications limit their use in fish culture primarily for the control of filamentous algae and stoneworts.

Certain types of algae produce compounds that cause a musty flavor or odor in fish flesh. These compounds are absorbed by the fish and can cause a highly offensive taste known as "off-flavor." This condition can be corrected within 3 to 10 days if fish are moved to water that does not contain these off-flavor compounds. There is no definitive evidence that thinning the plankton algae bloom with algicides reduces the incidence of off-flavor.

Shoreline Weeds

Water willow *(Justicia americana).* This is a good stabilization plant for larger lakes but is not recommended for small ponds because it spreads rapidly and could take over the water's edge.

Beware of **buttonbush** *(Cephalanthus occidentalis)* which may take up residence unannounced. This aggressive plant can expand into large stands in open, shallow water and become a problem. It grows wild here in southern Oklahoma.

Purple loosestrife *(Lythrum salicaria)* is another no-no and should never be planted around a pond, or anywhere else, for that matter. It is a serious plant pest. Infestations will crowd out native wetland plants and destroy wildlife habitat. A single plant can produce as many as 300,000 seeds in a season, which are carried by wind, water, and animals.

Floating Weeds

Floating weeds float in or on the surface of the water and obtain their nutrients from water rather than soil. **Duckweed** *(Lemna minor* and *Spirodela polyrhiza)* and **watermeal** *(Wolffia* spp.) are examples of common floating weeds.

Duckweeds (Lemnaceae family) are the midgets of the plant kingdom, the world's simplest and smallest flowering plants — just tiny specks of green on the water's surface. Having no true leaves or stems, they consist of only a roundish, flattened body called a frond. On some species, tiny roots dangle in the water.

A few duckweeds — if not allowed to get out of control — are not harmful to a pond, but a dense growth will block out sunlight, reduce oxygen levels, and destroy the pond's natural balance.

Never deliberately introduce duckweeds, but if you've got them, grass carp relish them and may be an effective control.

Emersed Weeds

Emersed weeds are rooted to the bottom but have stems, leaves, and flowers that extend above the water surface. They occur primarily on the shoreline and in shallow water up to 10 feet deep. Other common emersed weeds are water lily *(Nymphaea* spp.) and alligator weed *(Alternanthera philoxeroides)*.

Never introduce **American lotus** *(Nelumbo lutea)* into fishing ponds or shallow lakes — they quickly colonize shallow water and may engulf a one-acre pond in very short order. The beauty of the lotus plant was a favorite design of the ancient Egyptians and the very word *lotus* brings this to mind. American lotus is best known for its striking seed pods and — depending on your own imagination — may be thought to resemble a shower head, a pepper shaker, a wasp's nest, or even an ice cream cone! The pods are delightful in flower arrangements. Lotus grown in tubs is lovely for ornamental fish pools.

Water hyacinth *(Eichhornia crassipes),* a showy, South American floating aquatic plant of the family Pontederiaceae, should never be introduced into a pond or lake. It is a pernicious weed, though a beautiful one, and often clogs waterways in the southern United States. It is thought to have been introduced accidentally. Like lotus, it is desirable if controlled. The roots are long and fibrous, making this plant useful in spawning fish. If you want to spawn a few baby goldfish in your lily pool, this plant will give them cover.

Water primrose *(Ludwigia peploides)* is an annoyance in small fishing ponds and should never be introduced. This may sometimes happen by accident; if you find it growing in your pond, pull it out — preferably before it goes to seed.

Water fern *(Azolla mexicana)* is another plant that can completely cover a small pond in a short time and should never be introduced.

Floating-leaved pondweeds *(Potamogeton* spp.) are a large and important group of aquatic plants, but are not good for fishing ponds, despite their wildlife food value. They grow rampantly and invade deep water.

Water shield *(Brasenia schreberi)* is considered one of the worst pests in lakes and fishing ponds. Difficult to control, it can cover the entire surface of a pond in just a few years. Unfortunately, the gelatinous coating is protective and makes the plant resistant to herbicides.

Submersed Weeds

Submersed aquatic weeds grow under and up to the water surface. Most submersed weeds have flowers and seed heads that extend above the surface of the water. Examples of common submersed weeds include **hydrilla** *(Hydrilla verticillata)* and **Brazilian elodea** *(Egeria densa).*

Eel grass *(Vallisneria)* grows completely submersed on a hard mud bottom. It has long, single-bladed leaves and is an excellent producer of oxygen. Eel grass will attract walleyes and northerns during hot, calm weather.

Cabbage *(Potamogetonaceae)* is one of the best all-around fish producers, and will attract every species of game fish. Growing in the wild on a variety of bottoms, there are more than three dozen varieties in the U.S. It is submersed except for the small flowering tips, which extend an inch or two above the surface. It is an easy weed to fish because it is brittle and lures usually tear free with a quick snap. A technique for producing northerns is to throw a diving plug about 10 feet into a cabbage bed and crank it back to the boat.

Bladderworts *(Utricularia* spp.) are carnivorous plants. With their delicate leaves and dainty yellow flowers, it is hard to believe they are meat-eaters; but, in fact, they are known to capture and digest everything from mosquito larvae to small fish. Scattered along the branches, searching for unwary prey, are tiny bladders, actually hair-trigger suction cups. Hardly bigger than the head of a pin, the bladders — which are actually modified leaves — often appear dark red to black. Magnification shows them to be stalked and pear-shaped, with a small "trapdoor" surrounded by trigger hairs. In laboratory experiments, bladderworts have been shown to reduce mosquito populations; they have been proposed in some instances as a nonchemical alternative to pesticides.

With all their interesting qualities, however, common bladderworts are not recommended for introduction into recreational ponds. You may think it worthwhile to have some because of their interesting feeding habit, but do keep them in check.

Bladderworts provide shelter for fish and habitat for the small animal life upon which fish feed. They are of no importance to waterfowl. Common bladderwort has flowers ½ to 1 inch long. After flowering, they develop seeds in small capsules.

Water milfoil *(Myriophyllum heterophyllum)* in the wild provides shelter for small animals and feeding areas for fish. Although ducks dine on the fruits and foliage, in general this plant is considered a low-grade duck food. Water milfoil is seldom a problem in warm-water ponds but may grow excessively in spring-fed ponds or lakes, forming dense masses in the deepest part of springs. Their long, drifting stems may reach several feet in length. Water milfoil can become a pest in cool, deep, slowly moving water with a muddy bottom; care should be taken not to introduce pieces of this plant into cooler waters.

Fanwort *(Cabomba caroliniana)*, an exceptionally pretty plant, is often used in aquaria, but it is a nuisance plant and should never be introduced into a pond, as it grows rapidly and can quickly fill up a body of water. Fanwort occurs in the wild, but don't bring it home if you go fishing in other waters even though it supplies food and cover for many aquatic insects and fishes. The small white flowers, rising briefly above the water so pollination can take place, are very attractive. The flower nectaries are marked on each petal by a yellow spot at the base. These flowers attract a variety of insects — mostly flies, bees, and wasps — that pollinate the fanwort. If this plant is accidentally introduced into your pond and gets a head start before you realize it is there, grass carp readily eat it and may prove to be an effective control. In the wild, *Cabomba* grow up and form an umbrella shape fish like to hide under. But it makes fishing difficult because it clings to hooks.

Coontail *(Ceratophyllum demersum)* is another no-no because it can quickly crowd out other plants, filling the pond with a dense mat of vegetation. Fortunately, again, this plant is relished by grass carp, which are a promising natural control. Coontail is not all bad, providing as it does an important habitat for young fish, small aquatic animals, and aquatic insects — all part of the natural food chain. Ducks and geese like coontail, and it is a good water purifier. It can be an excellent fish producer if you fish lures and baits just over the tops of the clumps. Although it seems an unlikely source of medicine, it has been used as a purgative, diuretic, and remedy for biliousness and jaundice.

Management Methods

Aquatic weed control is a management plan that incorporates preventive methods such as proper pond construction and maintenance, biological methods such as the grass carp *(Ctenopharyngodon idella)*, and the use of labeled aquatic herbicides. The development of an aquatic weed management plan is dependent upon correctly identifying the problem weed(s) and selecting control methods that are compatible with efficient fish culture procedures.

Basic methods used to control weeds include preventive, chemical, mechanical, and biological techniques. Determining which of these is best for you involves consideration of the target weed species, fish production objectives for the pond, secondary water uses, and the cost of treatment options.

Preventive Methods

It is easier and less expensive to prevent weed problems than it is to control them once they develop. Careful pond site selection and careful pond construction practices are the first steps in preventing aquatic weed problems. Rooted aquatic weeds and algae usually begin growing in shallow water (less than 2 feet deep). Edges of new and existing ponds should be deepened so shallow water areas are minimized. The USDA Soil Conservation Service provides technical assistance for pond construction and renovation.

Fertilization is also an effective and economical way to prevent the growth of many aquatic weeds. Farm ponds are commonly fertilized to increase fish production capacity. Fertilization stimulates the growth of plankton algae. This algal growth is known as "bloom." The bloom blocks sunlight from reaching the pond bottom, which limits the establishment of rooted aquatic weeds. The key to successful control of aquatic weeds with fertilization is to establish and maintain a bloom before rooted weeds begin spring growth.

Decreasing the water level exposes shallow areas to freezing temperatures and drying and can effectively limit certain types of submersed weeds. For a drawdown to be effective, lower the water level in late fall and don't refill it until early spring. Some weeds, such as hydrilla and cattail (*Typha* spp.), are tolerant to drawdown and cannot be controlled by this method. "If you can't whip 'em, join 'em" is a saying often heard in our family. As we mentioned on page 52, cattails are not all bad; they have edible roots and other useful parts, and if not allowed to take over can be very useful.

Chemical Control

Herbicides may be used to control weeds in commercial fish ponds. The first step in successful chemical control is accurate identification of the problem weed. Weed identification assistance is available through county Extension and Department of Natural Resources offices. After the weed has been identified, select a herbicide that is labeled for commercial fish ponds. Read the herbicide label and make sure you fully understand it before applying the chemical to the pond. SRAC Publication No. 361, *Aquatic Weed Management Herbicides,* contains information on commercial fish pond herbicides (see *Sources*).

Herbicides should be considered only as a temporary control. Depending upon the herbicide selection and the weed species, they can be effective from a few weeks to several months. Long-term weed control can be achieved with a combination of recommended aquatic weed methods. For example, application of the proper herbicides followed by grass carp stocking will effectively control and prevent the reoccurrence of most submersed weed problems.

Controlling Problem Water Plants Nonchemically

Today, treatment with chemical herbicides is often chosen for water plant control. This does, in fact, provide a quick and effective way to clear large areas of aquatic vegetation. However, it has its drawbacks.

Mechanical Methods

Various types of aquatic weed cutters and harvesters have been developed for canals and large reservoirs, but these machines are impractical for fish ponds. Early manual removal of weeds by seining or raking will prevent some weed problems.

Chemical herbicides kill beneficial plants as well as nuisance species, and overdoses also can kill aquatic animals. The decay of massive amounts of plant material can lower oxygen concentrations to levels lethal to fish. Chemical control isn't permanent; treatment must be repeated indefinitely and can become quite expensive. And most important, chemical herbicides may have unknown long-term effects on the environment.

For these reasons it is recommended that pond and lake owners consider the following nonchemical methods for water-plant control. They are best suited for ponds, but a few (such as numbers 3 and 8) could be used in larger bodies of water as well.

1. **Black plastic.** Shading areas with large sheets of black plastic (8-millimeter thickness) will kill virtually all aquatic plants under them in 30 days. Float the plastic on the surface and anchor by fastening the corners to concrete blocks, or sink a sheet over the weed bed with weights. Be sure to puncture the sheet in a number of places so gases can escape.

2. **Weeding your pond.** Remove aquatic plants in a pond by pulling, digging, cutting, or raking. You can keep cattails, bulrushes, water willow, water shield, and water primrose in check by removing new growth. Weeding isn't a particularly enjoyable task (even on land), but it does work and it's safe.

3. **Grass carp.** This Asian member of the minnow family will, in some situations, control filamentous algae, duckweeds, and submersed plants. Stocking rates are still a matter of debate: Rates as low as 1 carp per acre have been successful, while some as high as 20 per acre have not provided the desired control. A reasonable ratio to begin with would be 3 to 5 carp per acre. See pages 66–67 for more on grass carp.

4. **Preventing introduction.** Problem plants often are introduced into ponds or other waters by unwitting humans. Serious pests such as water shield and lotus have been transplanted deliberately for their attractive leaves and flowers. Stocking fish, transferring boats, and emptying aquariums also have spread other undesirable

plants, both native and exotic. It goes without saying that any-one who wishes to keep a pond free of problem plants should take precautions with these practices.

If a new plant appears due to an accidental introduction, a quick weeding can sometimes head off a problem.

5. **Deepening the pond.** Any spot in a pond less than 3 feet deep invites aquatic plants. A shallow shoreline usually will be the first place invaded by an undesirable species. Deepening the pond's shallow areas may not eliminate all problems but will reduce their severity.

6. **Drawdown.** In a pond equipped with a drain, lower the water level temporarily so that aquatic plants are exposed and killed by drying.

7. **Blanketing.** Cover a portion of the pond bottom with a 6- to 8-inch layer of sand or fine gravel (preferably when the pond is under construction) to provide a plant-free spot. This is most appropriate for swimming or docking areas.

8. **Eliminating nutrient sources.** Feedlot drainage or residential sewage floating into a body of water practically ensures rampant plant growth. If possible, eliminate all such nutrient sources.

9. **Plant vs. plant.** Plants in a pond compete for nutrients, space, and sunlight, so a well-established species has an edge over an invader. Some plants may even produce chemicals that prevent the growth of other species. Although little research has been done in this area, it may be possible to keep out pest species by establishing other plants that can crowd them out or inhibit their growth.

The management of aquatic plants in ponds and lakes is an infant science. We don't yet know why a species will run rampant in one pond yet grow moderately in another, what keeps a healthy pond in balance year after year, or exactly how water plants influence each other's growth. These and many other questions remain to be studied, and the answers could lead to far safer and more effective control methods than what we have today.

Grass Carp for Pond Weed Management: Biological Control

The grass carp is a practical and economical control for certain types of pond weeds. Grass carp effectively control weeds with tender succulent vegetation such as filamentous algae and duckweed, but cannot control weeds that have tough, woody vegetation, such as water lily and cattail. Many states regulate the use of grass carp. Contact your Department of Natural Resources representative for guidelines in your state.

We have used grass carp in our own first pond with very good results and intend to place them in our second. They are not only efficient weed scavengers but also good eating. Grass carp were imported to the United States several decades ago because of their unusual ability to eat aquatic plants and the fact that they are excellent table fare. And, while they only occasionally bite live or artificial bait, they put up quite a fight when hooked. Though their initial cost is higher than a herbicide application, they are generally less expensive in the long run.

Grass carp may be used along with other weed-control measures, such as herbicides, or by themselves. Many pond owners stock grass carp for long-term control and use spot herbicide treatments to achieve immediate results.

Pond weeds are generally totally eliminated when 10 to 12 grass carp are stocked per surface acre. But this is *not* recommended in sport-fishing ponds, since some weeds are desirable as a refuge for forage fish from bass. Good results in sport-fishing ponds have been obtained when grass carp are stocked at a rate of 10 per *vegetated* acre. For example, a three-acre pond that is 50 percent covered by weeds is equal to 1½ vegetated acres and would take 15 grass carp.

If bass are present, then large grass carp must be stocked to ensure survival. Eight-inch-long grass carp are the minimum acceptable length for bass ponds; larger grass carp are recommended whenever practical.

There are several cases in which grass carp are *not* recommended.

- Sport-fishing ponds with less than 25 percent weed coverage. Use spot herbicide treatments instead to open up some areas for shore fishing.

- Ponds with tough weeds, such as cattails, bulrushes, and lilies. These usually cannot be controlled by grass carp, which lack the teeth needed to consume them.
- Ponds managed as resting and feeding places for ducks. Grass carp will eliminate plants favored by ducks for food. We feed our ducks pellets.
- Any situation in which grass carp could escape and enter public waters. This includes any pond that overflows, unless spillway barriers are installed. (See below.)

There are three types of grass carp from which to choose. **Diploid grass carp** are the recommended type for southern states. **Triploid grass carp** are equally effective at controlling vegetation, but are more expensive. **Hybrid grass carp** are not considered effective. Diploids will not successfully reproduce in ponds, as they require running water.

After stocking, it will be some time before you see any major results. Holes in weed beds may begin to appear late in the first year or early in the second year following stocking.

Restock at the first sign of weed regrowth. This will be after seven or eight years, which is the average grass carp life span.

Grass carp will escape over pond spillways and through overflow drains. Build parallel bar barriers to protect your investment and to prevent illegal escape of grass carp into public waters. Owners of large impoundments should confer with their county Soil Conservation Office to ensure that barriers will not increase the chance of a dam failure.

PART TWO

Fishing and Fish Farming

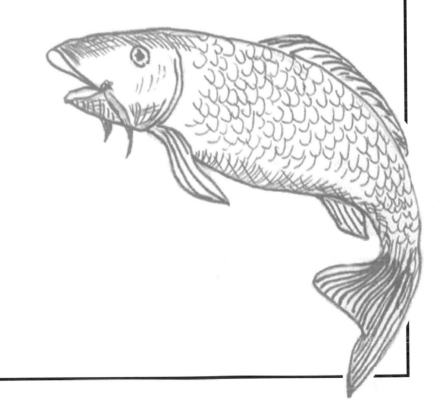

Chapter 5

FISHING DOWN THE MOONBEAM

ONE OF THE BEST THINGS about fishing is its utter simplicity — a beginner need acquire only a long stick, a length of string, a chunk of lead, and a plain old piece of cork to go with a fish hook, the only item that must be bought. Says Covey Bean, staff writer for *The Daily Oklahoman,* the old phrase "hook, line, and sinker" pretty well describes the necessities. And catching fish in your own pond is what pond building is all about — the goal you are working toward.

Most pond builders are well aware of the sport of fishing and can't remember when they didn't know how to fish, but to many newcomers the fundamentals of fishing are as mystifying as the basics of brain surgery.

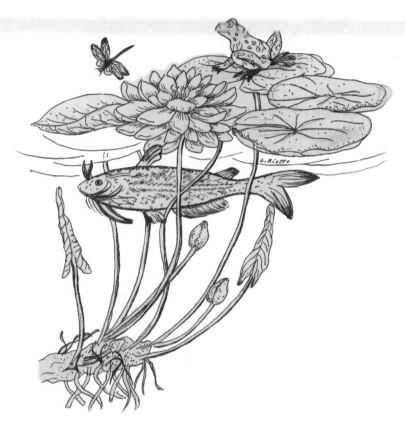

The food chain

Basic Gear

A beginner may need a little help. Today, any self-respecting novice — child or adult — should have a rod and reel plus a tackle box containing all the right stuff. The wrong stuff can complicate things, burning out a youngster and frustrating a grown-up. Don't insist on a high-dollar, bait-casting reel for your first fishing trip. In unskilled hands, it can be a nightmare of backlashes.

Purchase an inexpensive spin-cast reel, the kind with a closed face; they come filled with line. By merely pushing a button, anyone can put bait in the water pretty close to where he or she intended, and spin-cast reels do not backlash. While there are several different types on the market, my preference is for the original Zebco 33.

Don't worry too much about a rod, so long as the reel fits it. Buy something inexpensive and manageable, say about a 5-footer. For a child, get a short rod, something easy for a youngster to handle.

The basic fishing rig from the bottom up consists of the hook, a lead sinker clamped on the line about 8 inches from the hook, and a bobber snapped on the line a few feet above the sinker. The bobber floats on the surface, keeping the bait at whatever depth the line permits. Watch to see if it floats on its side; that indicates the bait is on bottom, and you should lower the bobber toward the hook. Casting a long length of line can be difficult — you might want to try one of the gadgets that allow the bobber to rise to a predetermined point on the line, making casting easier.

A beginner's tackle box — again, get an inexpensive model — should contain a supply of hooks, some bobbers, a supply of clamp-on sinkers, long-nosed pliers to remove hooks, a spool of extra line, a knife, and perhaps a stringer and a few artificial lures to make it look good. Beginners who want to catch fish will use natural bait — those who just want to play with their new gear can try the artificials.

Inside a Tackle Box

Fishing license (for anglers 16 and over; may vary)

Zebco 33 reel

Long-nosed pliers

50 No. 10 hooks

Clamp-on sinkers

Plastic bobbers

Fillet knife

Extra line

Rope stringer

Catching Fish

Sport fish such as black bass are a challenge even for experienced anglers. A beginner might be well advised to start with bluegills and other sunfish, which are found almost everywhere. They too are good sport: They bite readily and, despite their small size, put up a good fight. A bluegill the size of a man's hand is considered a nice one — a "keeper." Bluegills

Fishing for Trout

Here are some tips on fishing rainbow and brown trout, from the Oklahoma Department of Wildlife Conservation:

- Fish during the early morning and late afternoon
- Use an ultralight rod and reel spooled with 6-pound or lighter line
- For artificial lures, use small spinners, spoons, and crappie-size jigs (tube or maribou)
- Where legal, use live or prepared bait such as worms or salmon eggs
- Try small hooks (size 10 to 18) and sinkers to keep bait near the bottom and prevent trout from detecting any resistance
- Fly fishermen should use flies that resemble the insects and crustaceans that are most seasonably abundant
- Fish around structures such as behind large rocks and logs and below riffles
- Trout often congregate above and below waterfalls and in deep pools and undercut banks
- Rainbows tend to occupy faster-moving water, while browns are found in slacker stretches
- Trout face upstream to wait for insects to appear above them
- Fish tend to travel downstream from a stocking site (although some venture upstream)
- Fishing often improves a few days after stocking, when trout have adjusted to their new environment

have small mouths, so a tiny hook, say a No. 10, is necessary. You will find bluegills around weed beds, docks, under shoreline trees — practically anywhere they can find cover, providing, of course, the water you are fishing in contains fish.

Use the rod and your foolproof spin-cast reel to flip the bobber, sinker, and hook as closely as possible to the available cover. The bait will be taken down by the sinker. Watch the bobber — when it goes down, reel in your fish. This method will not work for every species, of course, but, depending on the bait you use, it will catch several kinds.

As you become more and more enthusiastic about fishing, you will probably go out and buy all kinds of expensive equipment — and then wonder why you don't catch as many fish as you did when the only gear you had was a hook, line, and sinker.

Bait

What will you use for bait? Minnows, crawdads, grasshoppers, chicken liver, shrimp, and crickets, as well as the time-honored worms, are all attractive to fish, but different baits will attract different types of fish. Here are some suggestions for best baits.

Best Bait

Minnows	Black bass, crappie, white bass, walleye, catfish
Crawfish	Black bass, catfish, walleye
Grasshoppers	Black bass, catfish, sunfish
Worms	Bluegill, sunfish, catfish, walleye
Liver, shrimp	Catfish
Crickets	Sunfish

The Microwaved Doughball

My son and his best friend had a lot of fun catching fish with dough-balls they made themselves — it just seems to add that extra something to your fishing pleasure if you give it the personal touch. David Brown, writing in the January 1994 issue of *Southern Outdoors,* claims that doughballs will tempt not only many species of sunfish but catfish and carp as well. And the bait, according to his recipe, is simple to make. All you need is a half cup of all-purpose flour mixed with just enough water to make it stick together. Though many anglers stop there, just putting a pinch of the raw dough on a hook, there is a better way. In this form it won't last long if you are fishing in bluegill-infested water — your pan-fish have a well-deserved reputation as bait-stealers.

Enter the microwave. If the dough is put in the oven for about 30 seconds, the mixture will cook more quickly and evenly. And the results are even better if the ball is flattened into a patty about ¼-inch thick. Test for doneness by pinching off a small piece: If the dough sticks to your fingers, cook it about 10 seconds longer. The quick cooking, unlike baking, yields a tenacious doughball that gels into a rubberlike consistency, making it easy to mold. And the bait is so resilient that often several consecutive catches are made using the same piece. Remold a little after each catch and drop it in again.

Flour and water, for the homemade doughballs, are the only ingredients actually needed, but adding a little extra something to enhance the odor doesn't hurt. Herbs and spices such as onion and vanilla, as well as oil-based salad dressing, create a scent trail that lingers in the water. We tried the time-tested anise and still think it the best fish attractant to put on bait. Scent on the doughball helps the fish find it if they don't immediately see it.

Chumming is another way to test a doughball's effectiveness. Toss in a handful of the tiny balls to see if the chum is devoured as it slowly descends. This also induces feeding activity, because when the fish taste something out of the ordinary they then search madly for the new food source.

Fishing by Telephone

This method was enough to make Ma Bell turn over in her grave — and she probably did! Back in the "wild old days," some inventive person devised a way of fishing by telephone. A hand-crank telephone current is an electric current induced by an alternating magnetic field. The telephone used was an old 5-bar-magnet phone with two 12-volt car ignition condensers hooked up to it, along with two long leads equipped with weights. These weights were tossed — one over each side of the boat — and then the operator cranked the telephone very slowly. Old telephones used were the early, large, wooden types, some equipped also with a small desk, and originally they hung on the wall. Two bells were mounted on them about 4 or 5 inches from the top. Can you imagine how strange this must have looked?

As the telephone was cranked, the catfish floated to the surface. They had to be retrieved quickly, because they usually would remain comatose for no more than a minute; then they would recover and swim away. Strangely, this operation would affect the largest fish the most, temporarily stunning them. Some as large as 35 pounds and more have been reported. But on the smaller fish it triggered an even more peculiar reaction: They would come out of the water and if the bank was gently sloping, they would try to climb it, moving very fast to get away from the electric current. In the days before telephoning the fish became illegal, people would be standing around with nets to catch the fish, and often there were a lot of them.

This device worked best, I am told, near a logjam or rocks in an eddy of a river. An eddy is a current of water or air running contrary to the main current, something like a small whirlpool. The boat was positioned fairly close to the shore. Old-timers have told me that this method would work only in a river; they had never known it to work in a pond, where there is little movement to form eddies. (This description is courtesy of my son, Eugene Achille Riotte.)

But there may be an exception. The waters of Lake Texoma — the largest man-made body of water between the Great Lakes and the Gulf of Mexico — are fed in part by the Red River, which separates Oklahoma and Texas. The heavy salt content in Lake Texoma, induced to some extent by the Red River, leads some to believe that it may be the reason that the telephone method and the "pacemaker" will work.

The pacemaker is the microchip successor to the old telephone technique. It is so small that it will fit into a matchbox or a sardine can. And it is so successful in stunning fish that it has resulted in hundreds of arrests for its illegal use.

Ma Bell must be whirling!

Keeping Bait Alive

Our family likes to live each day with gusto. Catfish will eat practically anything, but some mighty big ones, like the 17-pond channel cat Dwayne Sparks recently caught at Lake Murray (about 20 minutes from Ardmore), are caught on minnows (as reported in *The Daily Ardmorite* of April 24, 1994). It's no fun at all to collect bait and then have it die on you. Keeping live fishing bait cool is a major problem for many anglers and even more so in hot weather.

In a matter of minutes, critters like minnows, crawfish, grasshoppers, worms, and crickets can become overheated and will start dying. So here are some tips to ensure a supply of fresh, lively bait when you arrive at your favorite fishing place and later, as the day warms. To fish with gusto, you need live bait.

Minnows, of course, are the most difficult bait to keep alive, especially if you transport them for some distance. I got the following advice from Howard Sparger, a former game ranger and the author of many books on fishing. Some ice cubes and a plastic bag will work wonders for minnows. Punch several holes in the bag, fill it with ice, and tie the top closed. (If we are going any distance, we freeze ice in milk cartons in our own freezer in a solid block and chip it as we need it. Stored in our ice chest it keeps well, and also gives us cool drinking water for a day or two if we are camping with the trailer.) Lay the bag over the minnow bucket. As the ice melts, cool water will drip into the bucket and keep the water there from overheating.

If ice isn't available, wrap a piece of burlap around the bucket, wet it, and let evaporation do the cooling job. Or, if you find it easier, tie burlap loosely over the top and form a pouch that touches the water inside. Fill the pouch with several small rocks to weight it. Again, evaporation cools and the pouch will stir the water and help produce oxygen (very important). At your destination, don't just plop the minnows over the side of the boat and into the water. Surface water at certain times of the year is warm, and the minnows will go into shock if suddenly transferred from cool water to warm and will die almost immediately.

If you want to transfer them to warmer water, do so gradually by "tempering." This means taking several minutes to mix warmer water with the cooler water in the minnow bucket, allowing time for the minnows to become accustomed to the temperature change. When you have finished with this task, you can gain more hours of life for the minnows by lowering the bucket several feet down into cooler water.

Keep crawfish alive by placing a tray or two of ice cubes in the bottom of the bucket, then covering them with several folds of burlap topped with a thick layer of grass. Dump the bait onto the grass and keep the bucket out of the sun.

Worms are the easiest to keep alive, but also are easy to mistreat and destroy. Put them in a can with some dirt and mulch, and place the can overnight in your home refrigerator. When you go fishing, you'll probably take along an ice chest for cold drinks. Simply tie a plastic bag around the worm can, leaving a sharp loop of string. Hook this outside the cooler and let the can hang inside, suspended over the ice and cold drinks.

Crickets and grasshoppers can be kept alive the same way. The cold slows their movements and makes it easier to put them on a hook.

A handful of ice and a little ingenuity will solve most of your bait problems during warm weather and will help you "keep your cool" while fishing.

Using Herbal Scents to Attract Fish

Besides culinary and medicinal herbs, my mother's herb garden contained other, somewhat more mystical and unusual plants — herbal fish attractants.

Anise *(Pimpinella anisum).* According to my friend Jeanne Rose *(Jeanne Rose's Herbal Guide to Food),* the aromatic seeds of this plant are much used in cookery. They belong to a group she calls the "licorice" herbs because of their licorice-like scent. Evidently the fish like it too, for oil of anise made from the seeds, rubbed on bait, has long been used to attract them.

Lovage *(Levisticum officinale)* is a tall perennial herb that looks like a giant celery plant and tastes like one, too. The flavor is quite strong and the flowering tops yield a volatile oil — a scent fish seem to love.

Smooth sweet cicely *(Osmorhiza longistylis)* is another plant that fish seem to find irresistible. Quite probably this is because, as Louise Beebe Wilder tells us in her book *The Fragrant Garden,* the thick roots smell strongly of anise.

It's a "stinking" way to catch fish but it does work. Place some chicken entrails in a burlap bag, place in a lard can, and allow to age. Take the can to your favorite catfish hole, plant the contents in a likely spot, and get there bright and early the next morning. Catfish are quite remarkable at following a scent, and your reward may be a whopping string of hungry bullheads.

Recently, going through my pile of clippings, I found an article by Howard Sparger that I had been saving since 1986. According to Mr. Sparger, in 1981 a quiet fishing revolution began with the introduction of scents to use on artificial lures and live baits.

These were first developed by David Bethshears of Keeper Bait Company but anglers across the country soon began using them. Professional bass fishermen, whose livelihood depends on bringing fish to tournament weigh-in scales, were the first to tout the value of artificial scents. They observed that using scientifically formulated fishing scents gave them the edge of "a few more fish" day in and day out. The pros also found they were catching consistently bigger bass.

Then came news article after news article centered on how the olfactory system of bass and other fish species actually works.

These articles didn't recommend one brand of scent over another, but they did open fishermen's eyes. They began to think, "Hey, there has to be something to this. Now I understand why their olfactory powers are so overwhelmingly strong and why smell is so important to their every-day life."

Former skeptics quickly became convinced of these products' value — and some truly dedicated anglers today refuse to fish without one or more of them in their gear. If you haven't tried one, you might consider it; many companies now offer a variety of scents.

What is it about each specific scent — whether a natural product or an artificial one — that makes it beneficial? For instance, some of these products are designed only for soft plastics. They make artificial worms and grubs softer, so they have better action in the water and taste more real to the fish. Others are chemically formulated to initiate a feeding response in the fish you're after. One scent, a paste, is sold on the premise that it masks human odor, breaking down the fatty acids that are always on our hands. Other scents boast different characteristics.

When you think seriously about what a fishing scent should do, keep three important aspects in mind: First and foremost, the scent should taste great. When the bass or other game fish you're after picks up the lure sprayed with magic elixir, that fish should want to mouth it at least 1/10 of a second longer than it normally would, and, let's hope, for a lot longer than that!

Second, the longer a fish keeps a bait in its mouth, the better chance we anglers have to get a good, solid hook set, no matter what type of bait we're using. Third, the ideal fish scent should also mask a number of scents — human odor, gasoline, grease, among others. Scientists have proved that fish can be repelled by these and other scents they find offensive.

Chumming

"Chumming" also appeals to the catfish's sense of smell. Fish are cut up into bite-sized pieces and thrown on the water. Shrimp are also used for this purpose, cut up usually but whole if they are small. The fish and shrimp need not be in a state of decomposition.

Families Are for Fishing

My father, Rudolf von Helbach, came over from Germany at the age of 18 to join his older brother, Karl. At that time the largest state of Germany was Prussia, and my father always spoke of himself proudly as a "Prussian." The von Helbach family has been traced back to the year 1130. He once told me that the name means "clear" for *hel* and "brook" for *bach*. Perhaps that is why the family coat-of-arms is two fish facing each other, looking much like the sign of Pisces. (And the coat-of-arms of my husband's family is a white swan — another water creature — on a "field argent.")

My father and his brother entered into several business ventures. One of these was a large ranch situated on the Blue River near Durant, Oklahoma. This was the scene for much fun, and some of my earliest and fondest memories were of our two families fishing and picnicking by the river. Both my father and my uncle were well versed in fishing astrology, and we children were well instructed, learning both by precept and from practical application.

I have rarely known a woman who enjoyed fishing more than my mother did, and she was very adept as well, teaching my older brothers and myself. Our father was also a real expert. My mother, like my German father, had advanced ideas about how children should be educated. I was allowed to do just about everything the boys were permitted, and she usually participated as well.

She even let me go on nightly forays of frog-gigging with my father and the boys but did not go herself — that was where she drew the line. She was delighted to cook and dine on them, however, when we brought home a good catch.

Kids and Fishing

Today more and more families are finding that fishing is an inexpensive, relaxing way to keep youngsters happy. Get 'em started young!

Kids are easily entertained. Fishing allows them to be outdoors and to explore and learn about nature. And fishing doesn't have to be expensive. The only things necessary for a successful "kids included" fishing trip are a simple rod, a bobber rig, some bait, a stream or pond, and some enthusiasm.

Adults don't need to be expert fishermen to enjoy fishing with their kids. It can be fun for parents and kids to learn together. This happened in our own family. My lovely daughter-in-law had grown up in a family that didn't do much fishing, preferring other sports. But when Laura Elizabeth began toddling around the houseboat (with child-sized life jacket at all times) and wanted to "fish like daddy," Joan became interested, too, and was soon just as eager to go fishing as the rest of us. And now she is quite expert and very enthusiastic about pond building.

Here are a few guidelines to get kids started in fishing:

- Choose a location close to home, such as a farm pond, lake, or creek.
- Let the kids dig for their own bait, and here is a suggestion that can make this even more fun, especially in the fall. Fish are usually hungry the last few weeks before freeze-up, and to many fish, earthworms are a favorite bedtime snack. On a bright fall day, pick a moist, humus-laden spot and drive a stake 4 or 5 inches into the ground. With the back of the hammer, rub the wood so that it gives off dry grunts and calls up fishing worms. The curious or frightened creatures will obligingly come out of the ground.
- Worms are great for beginners, but other small live creatures that stay on the hook work well, too. A casual stroll through a field can produce crickets and grasshoppers, delicacies for panfish.
- Begin with spin-cast equipment that is fairly simple to use. Choose a rod that is lightweight and flexible, yet rugged enough to survive hard use. Rod and reel combos, many already filled with the line, can usually be purchased for about $15 and up.

- Purchase a few bobbers, sinkers, and hooks. The bobber determines the depth at which you fish, and a good beginning point is a foot above the sinker. Keep increasing the distance if fish aren't biting at the initial depth.
- To ensure a good time for all, keep your first few trips short and simple. Eventually, fishing will become a favorite pastime that the whole family enjoys together. We introduced our children to fishing at an early age, and they practically grew up with the sport.

Our Kids Go Carp Fishing

About the time my son was old enough to get a driver's license, he had run enough errands, sacked enough groceries, and mowed enough lawns to achieve his dream of owning a car — a beat-up old jalopy that he cared for lovingly. His boon companion, Tommy Childress, by similar means had acquired an old rowboat. We parents were so glad to have their teenage energy channeled off into something as innocent as fishing that we raised no objections, letting them indulge in their sport as often as school and chores permitted. Both boys were strong swimmers. And from time to time we mothers were gifted with wild yellow pond lilies!

I don't know where they found the fish, a large, golden-tinged species of carp (and definitely *not* grass carp), but I do know where they prepared the bait: as far away from the house as possible. This horrible-smelling stuff was a kind of dough and was formed into "stink balls." The boys put them in a can with a tight lid, a very tight lid. I saved used coffee cans.

The fish caught with this bait weren't all that great, either. They were large but so full of bones that eating one was like wading through a piscatory minefield. I gave up after preparing them for the table once or twice. (I now believe these fish may have been wild-type goldfish, *Carassius suratus,* a tropical variety. Ornamental goldfish sometimes thrive when their owners, tired of them, empty them into nearby water.)

Knowing exactly how to get around us mothers, the boys also took note while traveling happily from one fishing area to another of wild plum thickets, trees with wild possum grapes climbing up them, wild blackberry and dewberry areas, poke and other wild greens such as sour dock, wild lettuce, tops of wild beets, lamb's quarter, and wild mustard — to be marked and gathered each in its proper season.

Fishing Is Fun for Seniors, Too!

With careful thought and a small amount of equipment, fishing is a sport that can be enjoyed well into old age — and I mean really old age.

Herbal Fishing Lore

The juice of smallage (*Apium graveolens*) or lovage, mixed with any kind of bait, is said to attract fish as long as there remain any kind of fish within yards of your hook.

Wild ginger root was much used as a flavoring agent by the Native Americans of the Great Lakes regions. The roots were of particular value for strong-flavored meats and fish.

If you swallow a fish bone, it is said that it may be softened by drinking lemon juice and also white of egg.

The roots of sweet cicely, steeped, are also used for mixing with any kind of bait. Use half a dozen hooks on your line, tie bait firmly to the hooks, and fish will take the bait within many yards of your line.

Native peoples made a decoction against flies and mosquitoes by taking the leaves of garden pumpkins or cucumbers, pounding them and straining out the juice, and washing with this. The juice of mallows was also used. A modern mosquito repellent I have found useful when fishing is Avon's Skin-So-Soft. The repellent "secret ingredient" is red cedar oil.

My mother was still enjoying her favorite sport well into her 80s. Our City Lake, from which Ardmore receives part of its water supply, is situated within easy driving distance of our little city. After my father passed away, my mother made her home with my family. With the kids in school and my husband and I going to our respective jobs, she was often lonely during the day.

Often during the week, we would drive out early in the morning and help her to her favorite fishing spot on the lake, along with a comfortable folding chair, her equipment, a midmorning snack and thermos of water or coffee, and other small articles she might wish to have. As she could not walk very well and sometimes needed assistance, we also provided a bell so that the lake manager or his wife could help her if there was a minor problem. These very nice folks who loved fishing themselves were very obliging and often visited with her, for she was an interesting woman whose mental abilities never did deteriorate, and she kept up with the affairs of the world.

At noon we would drive out and pick her up. If time allowed we would clean her catch or otherwise care for it, and again arrange her as comfortably as possible for her afternoon rest.

At around 4 o'clock she would take her cane and hobble out to the kitchen and remove the casserole (often of fish), which I had prepared the night before, from the refrigerator, activate the timer, and place the dish in the oven. The children would be home from school at about that time and would prepare a vegetable or salad and set the table. When we returned from work, tired and hungry, there would be a nice hot meal waiting for us — almost as if by magic!

Plants That Stupefy Fish

My daughter-in-law is proud of her part-Cherokee heritage, showing up in her shining dark hair and large dark eyes. Talking with her father about the pleasures of her newfound sport, he entertained her with some tales of his own boyhood and of two herbs used by Native Americans for stupefying fish.

The first of these, **blue curls** (*Trichostema* spp.), a member of the mint family, is variously known as vinegar weed or camphor weed, and other names in different areas. **Wooly blue curls**, *T. lanatum,* is a shrubby plant, but most other species of the genus are herbs. The shrub is 2 to 4 feet tall, but the herbs range from 3 inches to 16 inches. The shrub has blue or purple flowers (rarely white) and more or less hairy leaves. The name of vinegar weed comes from the penetrating and acrid odor of the foliage of all species.

Native peoples made a decoction of leaves and flowers for colds, ague, and general debility; a bath of this decoction was taken against smallpox; leaves were chewed and put in the cavities of aching teeth; and fresh leaves were mashed and thrown in streams to stupefy fish. Blue curls is also a major honey plant in the western part of the United States.

The second plant he told her about is **wild cucumber** (*Marah* spp.), a member of the gourd family. Also called manroot and big root chilicote, this trailing or climbing vine has ivylike, thin leaves, and small, greenish-white flowers. Large, green, prickly seedpods pop open when ripe and scatter large brown seeds covered with a soapy pulp.

Native Americans roasted the seeds and ate them for kidney trouble. A decoction of the plant was drunk to treat venereal diseases; oil extracted from seeds was used for hair loss; crushed roots mixed with sugar were applied to saddle sores of horses; and the crushed pieces of green roots were put in streams to stupefy fish. Fish, unharmed, recover in a short time. The juice of the root is very bitter. The best habitat for this plant is streamside oak woodland.

He then told his daughter how he learned to clean catfish as a boy. "Catfish," he recounted, "are particularly firm and good to eat when caught in cold water, and when their dense, sweet meat is skinned properly, no taint of mud remains. The ordinary catfish may be skinned readily by first simmering the cleaned fish in boiling water for 1 minute, then cutting off the head and dorsal fin, and peeling the skin back to the tail like a glove. The skin is cut away but the tail is left intact to facilitate handling. The fish is rolled in cornmeal [once called Indian meal] and fried in deep fat until the flesh is tender and the outside golden."

Fish and fishing were very important to Native American agriculture, as we see from the famous story of "planting" a fish in each corn hill for fertilizer. Although it is expensive today, fish emulsion may be used for the same purpose.

Fishing by the Moon

Probably there is no other sport so surrounded by astrological fact and fantasy than fishing. Moon signers are enthusiastic in their belief that the phases of the moon influence their take when fishing or hunting. Others claim that it's pure lunacy. Somewhere caught in the middle are a whole bunch of people who don't know exactly what to think. And a lot of fishermen and hunters "believe" but don't want to admit it.

Even so, many in-betweeners wonder how a ball of dust and rock 250,000 miles out in space can possibly have an influence on Earth, and on the creatures of Earth.

But, without question, it has been proved over and over again that the moon does have influences on Earth. Each time it is "overhead," a high tide occurs on our larger bodies of water that is readily discernible. It occurs on smaller bodies as well, but is less noticeable. And many farmers and gardeners also believe it influences the water in the earth.

Opinions differ on which lunar phase and sign are best for fishing; however, most old-timers generally agree that the day of and the day after the phase change are usually best. Some say that the three days before and the three days after the Full Moon are also favorable, with the day after the Full Moon being the best.

From my book *Sleeping With a Sunflower* comes this bit of lore.

To Native Americans, each full moon of the year has a particular name and a story to go with it, and the various moons were named long before the settlers came to the New World. Two, in particular, were named for fish:

April's Full Moon has several interesting names — *Pink Moon* for the flowers (mostly pink) that covered the land at that time, *Fish Moon*, *Sprouting Grass Moon*, *Egg Moon*, and *Shad Moon*.

August's Full Moon has three descriptive names: the *Green Corn Moon,* the *Sturgeon Moon* (named for the fish), and the *Red Moon* (named for the heat and haze of the month).

The moon in Pisces and Cancer is considered good for both fishing and hunting, along with the association of these two signs in particular with eating and drinking. Possibly the appetites of fish are greater when the moon is in Pisces and Cancer, and when fish or animals are hungry, their tendency is to become careless — even the older and larger ones become less cautious. It is also believed that although fewer fish are caught in the sign of Scorpio, this is the best sign for trying for large fish. Usually these bigger ones have more fish "wisdom," but they get hooked just the same.

As to the time of day, many feel that fishing is best when the moon is directly overhead, and the two hours on either side of that time. At the New Moon, the beginning of the First Quarter (sun and moon conjunct), both the sun and the moon are directly overhead at noon (halfway between dawn and dusk). At the beginning of the Second Quarter (the sun and moon square), the moon is overhead at midnight (halfway between dusk and dawn). At the beginning of the Fourth Quarter (sun and moon again square), the moon is overhead at dawn, when the sun is rising.

The theory holds that the next best time for fishing is when the moon is straight "down" on the other side of Earth. This is midnight at the New Moon; dawn at the beginning of the Second Quarter; noon at the Full Moon; and dusk at the beginning of the Fourth Quarter. It should also be considered that the rising and setting of the moon varies as you go north and south.

In general, during summer the best fishing times are one or two hours before and after sunrise and sunset. Fish are also likely to bite before and after a warm front or a cold front moves in. In fall and winter, fish aren't likely to bite until warmed by the sun, making the hours from noon to 3 P.M. the most likely to give you a catch.

Fish are believed by many old-timers to be able to sense weather changes and to be particularly active three days before a storm. But on the day of the actual weather change, fish will not bite. This may be because winds often stir up the water, inducing the little fish to come out. And little fish are followed by big fish that prey on them. These, in turn, are followed by fishermen. Folklore further maintains that fish aren't likely to bite after heavy rains.

To be successful in fishing, it helps to understand fish. Let me give you a "for instance." A friend of mine who has a catfish pond feeds them regularly. He claims that they come in answer to his call when he approaches the pond at feeding time. This is not likely because a fish's sense of hearing is not keen, but they *are* very sensitive to vibrations, and have probably learned to associate food with the vibration caused by his individual footsteps. This may be the reason that, in certain fishing situations, quiet is important.

Fish depend heavily on their sense of smell, and as elsewhere noted, a sense of taste exists on the outer parts of their bodies. Also already noted is the existence of the sixth sense located in the *lateral line.* This is the sense organ that feels vibrations that are too low to be sensed by the human ear — and it is the lateral line that registers the vibrations from the footsteps of a person on the bank of a stream. Good anglers know that a footstep is more likely to frighten fish than is the human voice.

In *Astrological Gardening,* I have written extensively about my friend and neighbor Lucy Hagen, a prize-winning fisherlady who regularly competes with some of the most prominent fishing professionals in the United States. Lucy tells me that the tournaments at Toledo Bend Fin and Feather Marina in Texas are carefully set each year to occur on the best dates for fishing success. (The day my family fished on the Gulf of Mexico was also a good date for that year.)

Lucy is a bass fisherperson, and she likes to use rubber worms in every conceivable color, even striped and polka-dotted, but her first choice is a deep purple worm: For some reason, most of the fish she has caught have been on this particular color.

Lucy likes to use the "toothpick method." As the rubber worm is threaded on the hook, she thrusts a toothpick through the eye of the hook and then clips it flush with the worm on either side. This will usually prevent the loss of the worm and keep it from being pulled off the hook, mangled, or destroyed. She also uses anise oil rubbed *lightly* on the rubber worm to attract the bass.

I asked Lucy, who does a lot of night fishing with her companion, Mary Beth Knapp, about the effect of moonlight on fish and received a surprising reply: "When the moon is full and casts its light upon the water, fish down the moonbeam for the best results."

The Pesky Mosquito

Researching through my 1976 *Llewellyn Moon Sign Book*, I came across an interesting article on fishing by E. A. Lawrence about that bane of the angler — the pesky mosquito. According to Lawrence, fishing can be made more enjoyable by timing our activities to the cycle of the moon, and we can minimize our discomfort.

This is because the mosquito, like many other insects, is influenced by the moon (moths take their bearings by the moon when flying at night). Proof of this relationship was recently provided by Dr. N. H. Anderson of the department of entomology at Oregon State University at Corvallis.

Dr. Anderson has been catching insects in specially designed traps for many years. He reports that there are about one-fifth the mosquitoes flying about on nights when there is a full moon than when the moon is new or in its last quarter. Other entomologists have also reported that there are thousands more female mosquitoes in the air during the new moon than there are during the full moon. Scientists attached to the U.S. Army Medical Service and the U.S. Army Environmental Hygiene Agency corroborate this observation.

What these studies suggest, of course, is that rather than spraying ourselves with all kinds of dangerous pesticides, we should plan our summer-evening picnics and barbecues at times other than those days and nights when there is going to be a new moon. The best time for a relatively pest-free recreational event, according to these scientists, is during the cycle of the full moon.

I have mentioned elsewhere that Avon's Skin-So-Soft will repel mosquitoes, but it bears repeating. How nice! You can take a beauty treatment at the same time.

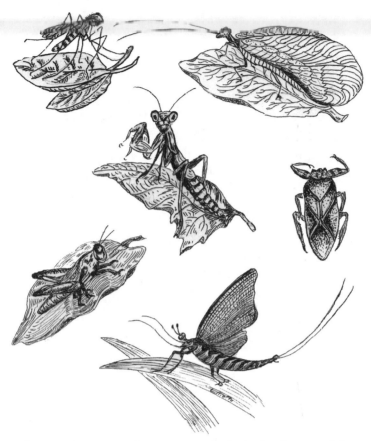

Insects that may be attracted to your pond, clockwise from top left: mosquito, lacewing fly, water bug, mayfly, grasshopper, and (center) praying mantis.

Weather Watch

Do different weather conditions really affect fishing? As with many other things, the answer seems to be both yes and no. Possibly we may find that the only point of agreement is that weather — any kind of weather — is sufficient excuse for poor fishing. One person will tell you that "a cold front hit and we didn't see any fish all day long." Another, "we had to fight a south wind (or a north, east, or west wind), and we had our poorest fishing day ever." Fish respond to the weather, all right, but we actually don't know much about how or why.

One factor that everyone seems to have ideas about is the wind. Does a wind from the south blow the hook in the fish's mouth, as the old saying would have us believe? Wind can be one of the most frustrating forces for an angler to contend with.

According to Al Lindner, author of *Catching Fish,* when a wind comes up, it is important to make quick, sound judgments about the kind of wind and waves your boat can tolerate. It may make sense to get off the water or find a sheltered bay.

When a wind is not a health hazard, however, as on a small pond, it often improves fishing. Wind cuts down on the amount of light penetrating the water, and it adds significant amounts of oxygen. Windy days seem to activate walleyes in particular, probably due to the increased oxygen. Even a gentle wind creates currents that can cause dramatic changes in temperature and move food sources around a pond.

What about fishing in the rain? We don't know how or why rain affects fish's behavior. One theory holds that during a heavy downpour, the beating of the rain on the water's surface helps to oxygenate the water. In some cases, large quantities of food can be washed into a body of water, causing the fish to begin feeding. Rain does not always trigger a feeding spree in fish, but it happens often enough to make it worthwhile to risk a few wet clothes to make a good catch.

Certainly if an electrical storm comes up while you are in a boat, you must *get off the water as quickly as possible.*

How much attention should you pay to barometric pressure, especially a falling barometer? Around here, you must pay close attention, for this is tornado country. I have lived through these violent storms all my life. Seeing the tornado funnel can be terrifying, but we learn to live with this possibility just as others in coastal areas learn to live with hurricanes.

Raise Your Own Fishing Worms

Called earthworms, angleworms, or fishing worms, these worms are found in warm and moist places throughout the world. The earthworm has a long, slender body that is covered with a slimy fluid. It is called "angleworm" and "fishworm" because it is a popular bait used by fishermen. Its body is divided into segments, or rings, and is red-brown in color. It ranges in length from ⅕ of an inch to several feet. The earthworm has no eyes. On each segment, however, there is a pair of spots sensitive to light.

The earthworm eats its way through the harder layers of soil that it cannot push through easily. It feeds on decaying vegetable matter. At night, it busily searches for fragments of leaves to drag into its burrow. The soil and waste pass out of the digestive canal and are left on the ground in little heaps called castings. These worms are also known as night crawlers.

The earthworm is not the young, or larva, of moths or other insects. It is a true worm that belongs to a group of segmented worms called annelids.

Here's How

To raise worms outdoors, a tight box 36 inches by 60 inches and 18 inches deep will be sufficient for several hundred worms. The exterior should be painted with tar and the inside can be waterproofed with paraffin. Embed the box in the earth in a cool, shady place that is well drained, allowing 3 inches of the box to project above the surface. A cover should extend several inches over the sides.

The Four Winds

When the wind is in the north
The skillful fisher goes not forth.
When the wind is in the south
It blows the bait in the fish's mouth.
When the wind is in the east
'Tis neither good for man nor beast.
When the wind is in the west
Then fishing's at its very best.

— Author unknown

Fill the box with fertile soil that is damp but not wet. Stock with worms, and cover the soil with decayed leaves, compost, or fresh sod. In dry weather, the soil should be moistened but not saturated. If dishwater is used, it will help feed the worms.

Raise earthworms indoors in a galvanized washtub or any other watertight container placed in a garage, basement, or vacant room and filled with fertile soil to a depth of 8 inches. After the soil is moistened, add 100 red worms. Next, take 1 pound of ground cornmeal and ½ pound of any kind of fat that has become rancid and can be salvaged. Mix this in the top 2 inches of soil. Feed the worms and moisten the soil every two weeks. This should produce 3,500 to 6,000 earthworms a year.

A simpler method is to make a compost heap with alternate layers of soil, garbage, leaves, and grasses. The worms will flourish in the soil around its base and may be harvested throughout the year with little attention.

If you raise your own, you can "open up a can of worms" any time you decide you want to go fishing.

Planting Worms

We once knew a farmer who raised earthworms commercially. Periodically he cleaned out his worm beds, replacing them with new soil and organic matter. When he called us we would take the truck, put an old tarp in the bed, and drive to his farm. For a small sum we shoveled up a truckload of the discarded soil, black and rich looking. We could hardly wait to spread it on the garden. We could not have done anything to make our garden more productive, for the discarded soil apparently still contained thousands of worm eggs that hatched and fed on the leaves we covered the garden with and tilled in during the fall of the year.

You might say we wormed our way to garden success!

Chapter 6

STOCKING THE POND

IT IS IMPORTANT to stock your pond correctly. A standard initial stocking of largemouth bass, bluegills, and channel catfish is recommended for all ponds one acre or larger with underwater visibility of at least 13 inches. Additional fish species may be added later, depending upon management objectives.

It is critical that correct numbers of each kind of fish be stocked. Improper stocking may prevent a pond from ever producing a quality fishery. According to the manual *Producing Fish and Wildlife,* the pond owner should stock 100 bass, 500 bluegills, and 100 channel catfish fingerlings per acre. These fish will usually not be fishable for two years. If larger fish are stocked, reduce the numbers. Stocking 50 8- to 12-inch bass, 100–250 4- to 5-inch bluegills, and 50 8- to 12-inch channel catfish per acre gives a pond a 1- to 2-year head start and minimizes mortality if an existing wild fish population is present.

Catfish alone are recommended for ponds less than one acre or for ponds with underwater visibility less than 12 inches. If only catfish are stocked, the number is dependent upon the turbidity. In clear ponds,

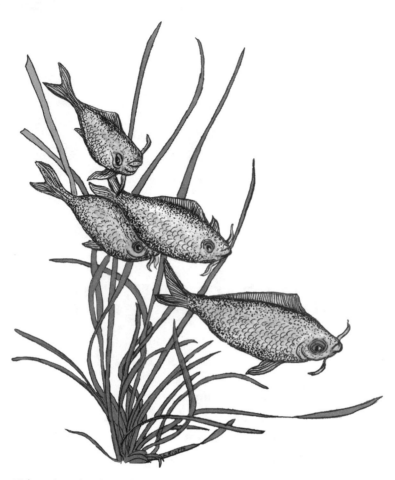

Fish swimming in sagittaria

200 fingerlings or 200 larger fish can be supported per acre. In turbid ponds, stock half this number.

To accelerate initial bass growth rates, it is recommended that 3 pounds of fathead minnows be stocked per acre when fingerling bass are introduced, or a year before adult bass are stocked. It should be realized, however, that fatheads will only sustain bass for a year or two, so bluegills must be stocked as well.

Some pond owners are reluctant to stock their waters with bluegills because of the fish's tendency to overpopulate. But bluegills are needed to provide food for bass; without them, a good-quality bass population will not develop. Bluegills are also fine sport fish if bass are able to contain their numbers through predation so that survivors grow to desirable size. Hybrid bluegills are mostly male, useful for stocking if overproduction is a problem.

Channel catfish in moderate numbers do not compete significantly with bass or bluegills for food or space. They can be considered a "bonus fish" in that they are not an important part of the predator-prey relationship. Bass and bluegills can function just as well with or without channel catfish present. By using all three species, though, the pond's potential to produce fish is more fully utilized. If properly managed, bass and bluegills need to be stocked only once. Channel catfish must be restocked periodically, since bass will eat almost all young channel catfish that are spawned.

Sources of Fish

A combination of fingerling largemouth bass, bluegills, and channel catfish — or catfish alone — can be obtained from the Department of Wildlife and Parks or from commercial fish growers.

To receive catfish alone or bluegills and catfish in the fall and bass the following spring from the Department of Wildlife and Parks, the pond owner must submit an application and an aerial photograph of the pond (available from the county Agricultural Stabilization and Conservation Service office).

Since rules may vary slightly from state to state, check with the Soil Conservation Office in your area to ascertain the correct procedure.

How We Stocked Our Pond

On the 20th of March, 1995, my son, Eugene, and I drove to the Claude Miller Fish Hatchery at Lone Grove, Oklahoma. Eugene had previously made arrangements, and our 600 catfish, placed in large, clear, plastic bags, along with five bags of minnows (for feeding the catfish), were quickly loaded into the pickup. Lone Grove is about 15 miles from Ardmore, and it took us about half an hour to drive back to the pond and release the fish.

They were very lively and quickly swam away. They ranged in size from 3 inches to as large as 7 inches. We watched carefully, and so far, we have never had any fish kill or sign of floating fish. The predatory white egrets (protected by law) may have taken a few. Eugene made a large feeding ring and they have quickly learned to come to it in the evening when my daughter-in-law, Joan, feeds them. This spring he made a second ring, because the first one appeared to be wall-to-wall with fish bumping shoulders, especially after we introduced 50 bass on April 4, 1996.

Bass are a predator fish. Before introducing them it is necessary to let the catfish grow to a good size so they will not be eaten. The predatory bass help keep the pond clean of trash fish brought in by the egrets, who often carry small fish in their bills as they fly from pond to pond. The cost of the catfish and minnows was $208 and the bass $80. We have had no losses from the bass.

We feed high-protein pellets and the feeding rings prevent the pellets from floating back to shore into shallow water. Even bags of fish pellets are getting more expensive. But, as I have previously pointed out: "It takes 7 pounds of grain to fatten a steer by one pound; a fish gains a pound on only 1.7 pounds of grain" (*Great American Food Almanac,* Harper & Row).

Releasing Fish — How to Temper

We purchased our bass from Dunn's Fish Farm in Fittstown, Oklahoma. They truck the fish in to Ardmore, in season, about once a month and sell them at a local feed store, filling orders. Here is how they suggest fish be handled:

1. To ensure survival, all fish must be taken to the pond immediately after purchasing.

2. All bags of fish must be held in a shaded area during transportation and while tempering them into your pond.
3. Upon arriving to your pond, *DO NOT PLACE THE BAGS IN THE WATER. Put them on the bank.*
4. Open a bag and slowly add water from the pond into the bag. Do this until the temperature in the bag is the same as in the pond. This process should not take more than three to five minutes per bag.
5. Take two fish out of the bag and release them into the pond. If they swim off, release the rest of the bag. If not, repeat step No. 4.

This firm offers Florida hybrid bass, largemouth bass (our choice), hybrid bluegill, fathead minnows, channel catfish, black crappies, and grass carp (white amur).

They offer a 24-hour phone service (see *Sources*) for information and consultation. They are a private firm and are not affiliated with the state of Oklahoma with fish or services.

To help prevent erosion and to keep the pond clear, Eugene, Joan, and Laura Elizabeth planted millet all around the pond's edge. The winds were so high that they put the seed in salt shakers, shielded it with their hands, and covered it as they went. We now have a bright green rim around the pond — enjoyed by both our older flock of ducks and our new ducks and African geese.

Chapter 7

CATFISH

IN THE CATFISH, Nature created a masterpiece and then packaged it to be one of the ugliest creatures alive. Wide-mouthed, bearded, and spiny, the **channel catfish,** *Ictalurus punctatus* Rafinesque, is a particularly fascinating creature and one of the most important species of aquatic animal commercially cultured in the United States. It belongs to the family Ictaluridae, order Siluriformes.

Life and Times of the Channel Catfish

In natural waters, channel catfish live in moderate to swiftly flowing streams, in large reservoirs, lakes, and ponds. They are usually found where bottoms are sand, gravel, or rubble, as opposed to mud or dense aquatic weeds. Channel catfish are freshwater fish, but they can thrive in brackish water.

During the day they are usually found in deep holes protected by logs and rocks. Most activity occurs just after sunset and just before sunrise. Young channel catfish frequently feed in shallow riffle areas, while the adults seem to feed in deeper water immediately downstream from sand-bars. Adults rarely move much from one area to another and are rather sedentary, while young fish move about much more extensively, particularly at night when feeding.

Age and Growth

Channel catfish grow best in warm water (and here in Oklahoma we can certainly provide that!), with optimum growth occurring at temperatures of about 85°F (29.4°C). They were originally found only in the Gulf

A catfish, close up

States and the Mississippi Valley north to the prairie provinces of Canada. Now channel catfish have been widely introduced throughout the United States and indeed the world.

In natural waters, the average channel catfish caught by fishermen is probably less than 2 to 3 pounds. The world record of 58 pounds was caught in Santee Cooper Reservoir, South Carolina, in 1964. In many natural waters, channel catfish do not reach 1 pound in size until they are two to four years old. One study in the Lake of the Ozarks, Missouri, found that channel catfish did not reach a size of 13 inches in length until they were eight years old. The maximum age ever recorded for channel catfish is 40 years. Most commercially raised catfish are harvested before they are two years old.

Physical Characteristics

One conspicuous characteristic of all catfish is the beardlike barbels around the mouth. The barbels are arranged in a definite pattern, with four under the jaw and one on each tip of the maxilla (upper jaw). The catfish's color, to a large extent, is dictated by the color of the water it inhabits. In clear water it may appear almost black; in muddy water it may be light yellow. Young channel catfish are irregularly spotted on their sides, but the spots tend to disappear in the adults.

Spawning

Channel catfish spawn when the water temperature is between 75 and 85°F (23–30°C), with about 80°F (27°C) being optimum. Wild population of catfish may spawn as early as February or as late as August; the length and dates of the spawning season vary from year to year, depending on the weather and the region.

Channel catfish are cavity spawners and will spawn only in secluded, semidark areas. In natural waters, male catfish — who take their responsibilities seriously — will build a nest in holes in the banks, undercut banks, hollow logs, logjams, or rocks. It is this behavior that necessitates the use of special containers in order to spawn channel catfish successfully in commercial ponds.

A Catfish As Big As a Man

"Well, the days went along, and the river went down between its banks again; and about the first thing we done was to bait one of the big hooks with a skinned rabbit and set it and catch a cat-fish that was as big as a man, being 6 foot 2 inches long, and weighed over 200 pounds. We couldn't handle him, of course; he would a flung us into Illinois. We just set there and watched him rip and tear around till he drowned. We found a brass button in his stomach, and a round ball, and lots of rubbage. It was as big a fish as was ever catched in the Mississippi, I reckon. Jim said he hadn't ever seen a bigger one. He would a been worth a good deal over at the village. They peddle out such a fish as that by the pound in the market house there; everybody buys some of him; his meat's as white as snow and makes a good fry."

From *Huckleberry Finn*, by Mark Twain (1885)

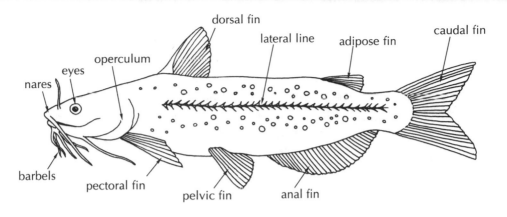

External parts of the channel catfish.

We solved the problem for our primarily recreational pond by placing a number of large used truck tires (preferably those really big ones used on semitrailers) here and there throughout the pond. These are large, heavy, and unwieldy, so we moved them with our Kubota tractor. Before placing tires in the pond, poke holes in them to release air and prevent floating.

The male selects the site and prepares the nest by fanning out as much mud and debris as possible. He will then defend this location against any intruder until spawning is completed and the fry leave the nest. The female is attracted to the nest and spawning occurs within it. She lays her eggs in a gelatinous mass on the bottom. After the eggs are laid, the male takes over and cares for them by constantly fanning them with his fins to provide aeration and to remove waste products.

Females spawn only once a year, in late spring, producing about 3,000 to 4,000 eggs per pound of body weight. Channel catfish usually become sexually mature at 3 years of age, although some may spawn earlier. In wild populations, they may not spawn until after the age of 5. After the eggs are laid, they will usually hatch in five to ten days, depending on water temperature. Water temperatures below 65°F (18°C) and above 85°F (30°C) will reduce hatching success.

Newly hatched fry have a large yolk sac that contains the nourishment they need for the next two or three days, until they are fully developed and are ready to start feeding. If father catfish "feels" an enemy approaching, such as an egret or a turtle, he takes them into his mouth. At night they return to his mouth until they are too big to get in. After the yolk sac is absorbed, the fry take on their typical dark color and will begin to swim up looking for food. At first swim-up, fry will gulp air to fill their swim bladders, which help them maintain and regulate their buoyancy.

Feeding

Feeding can occur day or night, and channel catfish will eat a wide variety of both plant and animal material. Usually they'll feed near the bottom in natural waters, but they will take some food from the surface. Based on stomach analysis, young catfish feed primarily on aquatic insects. The adults have a more varied diet, which includes insects, snails, crawfish, green algae, aquatic plants, seeds, and small fish. When available, they will feed avidly on terrestrial insects, and there are even records of birds being eaten. Fish become an important part of the diet for channel catfish larger than 18 inches in length, and in natural waters fish may constitute as much as 75 percent of their diet.

Channel catfish primarily detect food with their sense of taste. Taste buds are found over the entire external surface of the catfish as well as inside the mouth, pharynx, and gill arches. They are most common on the barbels and gill arches. In clear water, eyesight can also be an important means of finding food. The olfactory organs are found in the nostrils (nares), which are located on the top of the head just in front of the eyes.

A friend has a catfish pond on a ranch that she considers uniquely her own. No one but herself is allowed to fish there or feed the fish, which she calls her pets. Fish are very conscious of vibrations and they know her footsteps and approximate time of feeding, and are usually waiting for her when she approaches to cast the pellets upon the water. Once, just once, when the pond became a bit crowded, I was gifted with a big catfish. I was both flattered and overwhelmed, and eating it became almost a religious rite! I lighted candles and burned incense.

"The eye of the Master fattens His cattle" is just as true in feeding aquatic animals as it is with land animals. Observation is the key. All ponds produce some natural food for fish. And the quantity determines, in turn, the weight of fish the pond can support. Supplemental feeding is not usually required, unless harvest demand is high, or you desire large fish.

Catfish feeds are available as sinking pellets and as floating pellets. The big advantage of floating pellets is the opportunity to observe if the fish are eating the food.

Channel catfish are easy to feed, either alone or with other pond species. They learn quickly to eat artificial food, with a resultant growth-rate increase. A good rule is to feed both catfish and bluegills no more than they can consume in 15 minutes, up to a maximum of 20 pounds per acre per day. If fish are overfed, decomposition of wasted feed can

Spawning Trick for Recreational Ponds

As you might guess, the name "channel" catfish indicates that they do best in their natural habitat of running water, especially in the spawning season. After mother catfish has laid eggs, father catfish is aided in keeping them clean by running water. He can do this in a pond, but has to work a lot harder at his job.

My friend Buell Morris, who visited recently, told me about a way to use 5-gallon buckets with holes punched in them in the pond for spawning. With buoys marking their location, they can be pulled up. If there are eggs in them, the eggs are removed to a vat with a recirculating pump so the eggs can be kept clean until hatched. Living briefly in the vat, with no enemies, also gives the tiny fish an opportunity to grow a little and more chance of survival after being transferred back to the pond. When father catfish finds the eggs gone, he is likely to spawn again.

result in oxygen depletion, which will kill fish. Feeding should occur daily, or at least every other day, when water temperatures are over 60°F. Once you establish a feeding program, continue it throughout the growing season unless the pond's oxygen content falls below 5 ppm at the surface. When you stop feeding them, fish will lose weight.

The Thrifty Fish Feeder

The "thrifty fish feeder" will keep feed from being wasted by washing into weeds or to the shoreline, where it may decompose. By observation, you will quickly determine just how much feed the fish will consume in 15 minutes, fish will be fed just enough to keep their growth rate constant, and no feed will be wasted. (Courtesy of Buell Morris)

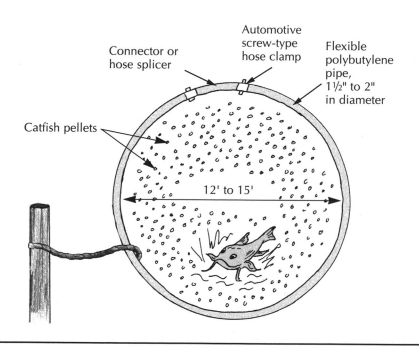

The "Supersenses" of the Catfish

The catfish has more senses than humans have, according to Jean George, author of *Marvels and Mysteries of our Animal World*. With his "supersenses," he hears the sound of young crawfish stirring in their mother's apron, "feels" the dying minnow in the faraway pickerelweed, senses whether he is swimming right side up, and sees far above him a distorted kaleidoscope of trees and boats.

Taste. Covered with taste buds, the fleshy barbels, usually eight in number, hang down like a beard from his jaw, and constantly "sip" the mud for flavors. These whiskers bring to the catfish the taste of sticks, flies, snails, weeds, and even rusty cans, which he savors not only with his barbels but also with his scaleless body and tonguelike tail. And the ever-hungry, undiscriminating catfish can be caught on just about anything, including a shred of watermelon rind, a piece of leather, an old bone, even a button!

Catfish are often caught with baited trout lines. My brothers used to do this and they would make big catches even in water roiling red with mud and sticks. Smell, like sound, travels quickly in water.

Hearing. The catfish is tremendously sensitive to vibrations transmitted through air, ground, or water, and can hear the cautious step of the fisherman walking on the bank. You must be very, very quiet. Even so, it will probably hear you when you approach the pond.

The "Lateral Line." You will see this stripe or design when you turn a fish on its side. Attached to this tube of mucus are nerves and pores, bringing to its owner sensations that we will never understand, bringing as it does the "touch" of things far away. A sort of thermostat, it informs the fish how many degrees the water has warmed and how long to remain quiet until his body has adjusted and he can move to a higher and warmer area. This is how the catfish knows when to move upstream with the spring season

Chapter 8

RAISING FISH COMMERCIALLY

"AQUACULTURE, the production of aquatic animals and plants," says Dr. Marley Beem, aquaculture specialist, "is the fastest-growing form of alternative agriculture in the United States today." You might say it's the wave of the future.

The imagination of people across the country is often captured by intriguing pictures of eagerly feeding fish, and they sometimes get carried away in a burst of enthusiasm for fish farming. It is not my intention to pour cold water on anybody's hopes and dreams but rather to temper enthusiasm with an objective look at the benefits and disadvantages involved in fish farming, North or South, on a commercial basis.

Before jumping in to fish farming, warns Dr. Beem, it is wise to consider four steps to profitable aquaculture: learning, evaluating, planning, and testing.

First, learn all you can about aquaculture. Start by contacting your local County Extension office; staff there will have information

Aquaculture researchers and Extension specialists in the North Central Region report that rainbow trout (left) are the most suitable for fish farming, with the attractive hybrid striped bass (right) in the middle range.

appropriate to your region. They have been trained to respond to questions about aquaculture and can direct you to other sources, if necessary. Seek information from potential customers, Soil Conservation Service employees, businesspeople, and others. Visit working fish farms, both private and public. Talk with experienced fish farmers. Subscribe to aquaculture periodicals. View videos on the subject. Attend aquaculture workshops, seminars, and conferences. (This is good advice as well for those planning a recreational pond.)

Next, says Dr. Frank R. Lichtkoppler, of Ohio State University, evaluate your resources — human and natural. Consider if you have the time, energy, and financial resources to develop a fish farm. Do you have adequate land and water that can be used for fish farming? What equipment will you need? Being a knowledgeable fisherman is not necessarily the best background for running a successful commercial operation. Actually, farming is the best experience for getting into fish production. Fish farming is agriculture, and therefore requires close management, hard work, and the ability to tolerate risk. Basic farming skills like operating a tractor, equipment repair, and welding are needed far more than fishing experience.

Third, just as you would plan a farming operation, it is necessary to plan your aquacultural enterprise. Develop a business plan. Check for potential pitfalls. What permits are needed to raise fish for sale? If you hope to obtain outside financing for your enterprise, a business plan is essential.

Fourth, test your plan on a scale that you can afford. Are you able to grow fish on a small scale? What works? What doesn't? Build your business after you have worked out the problems in your plan and as you gain knowledge and skill as a fish farmer. Make sure you can grow and

Early Aquaculture

"The first fish farmers in America were the Hawaiians. When Captain Cook landed at Kauai in 1778, he counted 360 fish ponds—covering some 6,000 acres and producing about two million pounds of fish per year." From *The Great American Food Almanac* by Irena Chalmers with Milton Glaser and Friends, published by Harper & Row, New York (1986).

sell the fish before you invest large amounts of time and money on production.

Things to Consider

Land, water, capital, a market, and management skills are requisites for successful fish farming. A good working knowledge of these things will help you plan and develop your enterprise.

How Much Land?

One or two acres of water — which may be sufficient for a family recreational pond — will not be adequate for a full-time fish-farming operation. A small trout raceway operation capable of producing up to 100,000 pounds of fish may require 16 pairs of tanks that are each 35 feet long by 6 feet wide. To generate $10,000 in income from a bait minnow farm, one would need a minimum of 20 acres of ponds, each acre producing $500 net income. Land for a fish farm must usually be improved before it can produce. Construction of ponds, wells, work and storage buildings, and hatchery facilities will be necessary. Make sure the land that you want to develop does not have detrimental restrictions. A wetlands designation or zoning and deed restrictions can make land difficult, if not impossible, to develop. Pesticides or other chemical residues on the land may make it unusable for aquaculture. To hold water, pond development requires clay soil. Soil tests will help tell you if your land is suitable for pond construction. You can get help on pond construction from your Soil Conservation Service. This applies to a recreational pond, also.

Big mistakes are expensive, warns Dr. Marley Beem — there is no good use for facilities built the wrong way or on the wrong site. The most common errors are ponds that will not hold water and ponds that cannot be drained.

But let's look at the bright side as well. In spite of problems, many of which can be overcome, established fish producers will tell you that fish farming is a great way of life. Being tied closely to the land and living out the seasons make countryside life a rewarding adventure. Fish farmers experience a deep sense of pride and satisfaction as they watch their fish feeding, growing, and finally being harvested. And in well-managed ponds, more meat per acre can often be produced than by leaving the land in pasture for cattle.

Clean Water Is a Must

Water quality and quantity are critical. Bass, in particular, will not do well in muddy water. The water should be void of any chemicals harmful to fish. Underground water from wells is preferred for fish farming. Springs also are usually free from wild fish and parasites. To a large extent, water temperature will determine what species of fish you will be able to grow successfully.

Rainbow trout — the very name sends a thrill of excitement to both those who who fish and those who dine on them — grow best at between 55 and 68°F. Stock when water temperatures stay below 70°F.

The amount of water available will limit the size of the fish farm. At a minimum, you want enough water to drain and fill a fish production pond at least once a year, as well as the capability of replacing any water lost through leakage or evaporation. For a 20-acre pond averaging 4 feet deep that loses 1 foot of water per year, you need 100 acre-feet of water per year. To produce 100,000 pounds of trout in a raceway culture system without recirculating the water requires a flow of 500 gallons per minute. A recreational pond may also need a well in times of drought.

Remember that the most important ingredient for fish farming success is water quality. Cooperative Extension Services in most states offer water quality workshops for fish farmers. These let the prospective fish farmer get hands-on experience using test equipment and learn what the water quality numbers mean and what management actions to take.

New fish farmers who put off buying and learning to use test equipment often sail along happily believing the warnings do not apply to them. Then suddenly they discover an entire pond of dead or sick fish. Producers who take the time to check oxygen, ammonia, nitrite, and other water quality factors on a regular basis find that the effort pays off in many fewer fish kills and disease problems.

You Will Need Capital

Aquaculture is capital-intensive. You'll probably need financing to construct ponds, raceways, wells, and buildings, and for other specialized fish production equipment. Capital investment for a 100-acre bait-fish farm is estimated to be $171,000, varying, of course, from area to area. Establishment costs for a small trout hatchery capable of producing 36,000 pounds of fish per year is estimated to be $26,400. Feed and labor costs are variable expenditures in the production of trout, bass, and other aquatic species. Because aquaculture is a type of farming, agricultural lending institutions are more likely to finance it than are commercial banks. To obtain financing for fish production, remember that a business plan is normally required. Aquaculture is a business: To avoid failure, make sound financial plans.

It is important to take time to develop markets and find out what your customers need. As you acquire more knowledge of current conditions, you may discover a more profitable market for your product than the one you had originally planned. Then you must change your way of growing and harvesting to fit the new market. As people become more health conscious, they will continue to eat more fish. Fish produced under controlled conditions are likely to be cleaner and healthier than those caught in a stream, which may be polluted by something several miles away that you are not aware of.

Markets

To be successful, fish farmers must be proactive, says Dr. Lichtkoppler, in marketing their products. Research in the north-central region of the country has demonstrated that there is a perception that farm-raised fish are fresher, healthier, and of higher quality than are wild-caught species. Emphasis on careful handling, cleaning, process-ing, packaging, transport, and retail sales is important in order to develop your market. Research funded by the North Central Regional Aquaculture Center (NCRAC) indicates that fish farmers in that area can market their farm-raised fish as a high-quality, highly valued prod-uct. These farmers must look to develop niche markets where they can sell limited quantities of high-value products. This will take time and determined effort.

What Kind of Fish?

What kind of fish should you produce? Consider the difficulties involved in the rearing of each fish species. If you are just learning the business, start with the easiest fish.

Aquaculture researchers and Extension specialists within the north-central region were asked their opinions on the suitability of the various fish species for commercial agriculture. In general, they agreed that bait minnows, rainbow trout, hybrid sunfish, bluegill, and bait fish were the easiest. Largemouth bass, hybrid striped bass, crappie, chinook salmon, brown trout, and yellow perch were in the middle range. Brook trout, smallmouth bass, northern pike, and walleye were thought to be the most difficult. This would apply also to a recreational pond.

Bait Fish

Golden shiners, fathead minnows, and goldfish are among the most popular bait species and can be produced reliably in ponds, according to Dr. Beem. These species reproduce naturally and grow well on inex-pensive feeds. You'll need a series of flat-bottomed ponds that can be drained, seined, and refilled so buyers can be supplied on a regular basis. If you are considering bait-fish production, key requirements include a site suitable for levee ponds and 20 or more gallons of water per minute per surface acre. The investment for a 100-acre bait-fish farm is in the neighborhood of $200,000.

Largemouth Bass

The largemouth bass *(Micropterus salmoides)* is one of several "basses" that are actually members of the sunfish family. White bass and striped bass are examples of the true bass family.

Striped bass, hybrid striped bass, and red drum for food are newly developing species for fish culture. Farms are concentrated somewhat along coastal areas. The Florida bass is a distinctive subspecies of largemouth bass but will blend genetically with the northern species. Although the two strains differ slightly in body structure, behavior, and growth, biochemical tests are necessary to identify them positively.

Largemouth bass are of value to fishermen chiefly because of their feeding behavior. They are voracious predators that readily strike artificial baits. Bass begin to eat fish when they are about 2 inches long. They swallow live fish and other aquatic life whole rather than bite off chunks, which limits the size of what they can eat. Because of this, we introduced bass fingerlings in our own catfish pond several months after introducing the catfish fingerlings. At the time we introduced the catfish, we also put in several bags of minnows, which bred at frequent intervals.

The availability of adequate-size live food (bait fish or forage) usually limits bass growth. With adequate forage they can surpass 2 pounds the first year, but normal growth is about ¼ pound a year. Mature females grow larger than males, with northern strains growing up to 10 pounds. Florida strains and first-generation crosses with northern strains can reach more than 20 pounds.

Largemouth bass will eat a variety of live fish, but bluegill are a particularly important food because they reproduce throughout the warm months. This furnishes a continuous supply of different-size forage fish. Tilapia and/or goldfish are commonly used as forage on fish farms because more can be produced at lower cost. About 5 pounds of live forage is required to add 1 pound of gain to a largemouth bass.

Largemouth bass do not grow well in muddy ponds because they feed by sight. Water clarity should be at least 8 inches and preferably 12 inches. This applies to recreational ponds as well as to fish farms.

Largemouth bass, bluegill, and other sport-fish fingerlings are widely produced for stocking recreational ponds. Key requirements include land and water resources for levee or watershed ponds. You'll need special skills to handle, protect, and provide food for very young fish. Gain experience in producing large fish before you attempt the production of fingerlings.

Trout

Rainbow trout farming in the South centers on the Great Smoky Mountains of North Carolina, Tennessee, and northern Georgia, where water from mountain streams is diverted to flow through concrete raceways and tanks. A small farm is one with a water flow of 500 gallons per minute. The start-up cost for such a small farm is approximately $26,000.

Trout are a fish of northern waters, related to the salmon. Most kinds of trout live in northern lakes and rivers, and those that live in the sea run up the streams to spawn. Trout are an important food fish and many fishermen's favorite game fish, along with salmon. All put up a good fight when they are hooked. They are very greedy eaters.

Scientists divide trout into two main groups, the *black-spotted,* or *true trout,* and the *chars.* True trout, including rainbows and steelheads, belong to the same genus as the Atlantic salmon. The chars include the brook or speckled trout, the California golden trout, and the Dolly Varden.

Trout thrive best in cool, clear waters with a gravelly bottom, where the current is strong and there are rapids and deep pools. The fish spawn in the cold weather of fall or early spring. The eggs hatch when the water temperature rises in the spring. The eggs can be kept on ice and shipped to all parts of the world. During winter, the fish may go down the rivers and into the open sea. They often remain for many days in the mouths of rivers or in small bays along the coast.

Catfish

Catfish is the major aquaculture product in the South. Farms are centered in Mississippi, Arkansas, Alabama, and Louisiana, although smaller industries exist in most other southern states.

Catfish farming is divided into fingerlings and food fish production. Many producers specialize in one or the other. Primary requirements for levee pond catfish farms include 25 gallons per minute of water for each surface acre of pond, and land suitable for levee ponds. The investment ranges from $3,000 to $5,000 per surface acre, excluding land costs.

Key land and water requirements for watershed pond catfish farms are similar to those for recreational ponds but include considerably more land and water, of course. You'll need to invest from $2,000 to $4,000 per surface acre, excluding land costs.

Dollars and Sense

Taking the plunge into aquaculture should be done only after careful planning. This may not be as complicated as you think. A good way to start is to list the income and expenses you expect. First, consider the income your fish farming operation will produce. Generally, this means estimating the amount of fish you will produce and the price you will receive for them.

Next, make a list of the expendable items you will need to buy each year to produce your fish. This will include feed, fingerlings, labor, fuel, electricity, equipment repair, interest on borrowed money, etc. These are your variable costs.

Finally, make a list of costs for everything associated with machinery. Examples include pond construction, wells, pumps, trucks, feed bins, tractors, aerators, and buildings. Do not overlook the cost of buildings, tractors, or other equipment that is already purchased. They should be charged off some each year of their expected life, since they will eventually need to be replaced. Equipment used for other jobs on a farm also needs to be partially charged so each enterprise can stand on its own. For example, a tractor that is used 20 percent of the time for fish farming would show up on your list as 0.20 tractors. You may wish to look over published fish farming budgets available through your county Extension agent to ensure that your listed expenses are complete.

One major reason to estimate income and expenses is to be able to project your return or profit. Another use of the numbers is to project a break-even cost for what you produce. To get these critical numbers you will need to organize your information into a form known as an enterprise budget. Your numbers are already divided into three lists: income, variable costs, and fixed costs. Now put these numbers into four columns: item, quantity, $/unit, and total.

Do not get discouraged if the estimated return is very small or even negative. The first budget is just a starting point. Think about ways to reduce your costs, such as doing your own pond construction work with used equipment. This could reduce pond construction costs by half. Another way to save money is to use your own funds without borrowing. A third way is to expand.

But let's also look on the bright side. In return for their efforts, fish farmers enjoy an independent, countryside lifestyle and can expect to receive a reasonable return on investment, similar to many other forms of agriculture. In well-managed ponds, more meat per acre can often be produced than by leaving the land in pasture for cattle.

The von Helbach family (my father's family) coat-of-arms seems especially appropriate for us fish-lovers

PART THREE

Other Pond Dwellers

Chapter 9

DUCKS — AND GEESE — IN A ROW

TODAY I SPENT a happy morning at the pond watching my son install a bug zapper on a tree on the island. To do this he had brought down our small boat, pulling it on a small trailer, with our all-terrain Kawasaki, a compact little vehicle intended for off-road use, which is handy for pulling feed, fertilizer, or implements on a trailer, saving numerous trips and carrying.

As I watched, my attention was more and more attracted to the amusing antics of our ducks. The perimeter of the pond has a varied growth of Bermuda, wheat, rye, and other grasses. My son had been telling me for several days that the ducks, for some unknown reason (still unknown!), chose to feed on the wheat heads in one particular area. As I watched, the flock swam to the area and began to feed. They stretched their necks to the utmost, barely making it, pulled down a wheat stalk, fed on the grain, let go, and selected another one, feasting for about half

Our hybrid white Pekin ducks are large, and a great improvement over older types. Our gentle African geese take feed from our hands and are very careful not to nip our fingers. They are very beautiful, with dark wings and a line of dark feathers running from their heads down their long graceful necks to the back. Bills are a soft gray.

an hour and then returning to the pond to resume swimming. Day after day they have come to this same spot — we don't know why.

Ducks eat insects, snails, frogs, and fish, but we also feed ours pellets, and sometimes they eat some of the catfish pellets as well or avail themselves of the insects killed by the bug zapper. The ducks we prefer to keep are the large hybrid white Pekins. We make no effort to propagate them, but occasionally a mother duck will build a nest, line it with the down from her own breast, and hide it somewhere. We get a surprise on the day she leads her ducklings down to the water, which is just as soon as they can travel.

We enjoy our ducks mostly for their beauty, funny habit of swimming "ducks in a row," and their friendliness, for ducks also make amusing pets. But they do produce a useful product as well — duck eggs. Many people turn up their noses at the mention of eating ducks' eggs but we like them. And they, being so large, are just wonderful for baking purposes — especially cakes.

My first adventure with ducks came about during World War II. My husband was called to Hanford, Washington, to work at the atomic bomb plant, and I was left alone with two small children. Before he left

Duck Eggs For Baking

Duck eggs make a fantastic cake: rich, fine-textured, rising high and prideful. One of the secrets of success is in timing the beating of the egg whites. Since they tend to deflate if they stand around for any length of time, *The Fannie Farmer Cookbook* recommends that you beat them last, just before they are folded into the batter. Try it. Their volume is important. How long should you beat? You've finished when a whisk or beater removed from the mixture pulls with it stiff peaks of egg white that have a shiny, glossy surface.

When my recipe calls for three whole eggs, I use only two if I am cooking with duck eggs, and otherwise follow directions.

he had dressed out all the chickens and put them in the freezer, and I wanted to raise a younger flock for better egg production.

I went to the hatchery and bought two dozen chicks and a dozen white Pekin ducks. Earlier I had cut a large cardboard box lengthwise, strung an electric cord to accommodate two lightbulbs for warmth, placed waterers, and filled feeders. I happily brought home my chicks and ducks and the kids and I had a lot of fun putting them in their "palace" and watching them avail themselves of water and feed.

For about a week or so all went well. The ducks were "messy" and the newspapers had to be changed frequently, but that posed no problem. What did, however, was the simple fact that I had not realized that the ducks would grow faster than the chickens. They did, and completely without malice they stepped all over the baby chicks. In a few days the chicks accommodated to the clumsy little ducks and began growing rapidly as well.

I had put the cardboard box in a small outbuilding formerly used as a stable for our milk goats, but when both ducks and chicks grew larger, I transferred them to the regular poultry house. With more room, things quieted down.

"Duck Liberation Day"

In the spring of 1995 my son, Eugene, and my granddaughter, Laura Elizabeth, drove to the hatchery about 14 miles away. Laura Elizabeth had a great time choosing "her" ducks. They brought them home and followed much the same procedure for raising them as I had done many years ago. All went well.

My son had kept a small flock of ducks for several years, letting them swim on the small pond. Eventually, though, they would all disappear, killed at night by stray dogs or coyotes.

When we built our new, larger pond, my son planned for an island with a twofold purpose: to save a beautiful large oak tree and to be a home for the ducks, providing them with some degree of safety. He placed a shelter for the ducks on the island, and put up a temporary fence. When we deemed them to be of sufficient size, the ducks were transferred to their island abode. We gave them a week or so to get accustomed to their new residence.

The Riotte family just can't do anything without a celebration, so we planned carefully for "Duck Liberation Day." My son sketched out a scenario and everybody had a part (and each took a turn as videographer). The ducks, which had been confined in the house, were let out one by one so everybody had a chance to have his/her picture taken holding a duck. Then we took turns as each family member was photographed taking down the fence to "liberate" the excited — but somewhat bewildered — ducks. At first they didn't seem to know what was expected of them, but gradually they picked up courage and ventured out on the water — swimming a few minutes, then rushing back to the island. Ordinarily, when the eggs of a mother duck hatch, she leads them to the water as soon as they can walk. Ducks aren't terribly bright but the reasoning behind our plan was to teach them that the island was "home" and that they could spend the night there in safety. Eventually they got the hang of it and began joyously swimming farther and farther out on the pond.

All the time that this was going on, the barbecue was wafting its fragrance toward us, so we soon left the ducks to their happy celebration and went back to the living room and replayed the video. Unlike many home videos we had made in the past, it had turned out very well. Picture, sound, color, and scenes were all very good. We have enjoyed replaying it many times since — and it will grow more precious with the years.

In June 1996 we had another "liberation day" for the ducks and geese raised that spring. They had been moved progressively from the cardboard box in the laundry room, to the storage building (where a snake got in and had to be killed), to the former dog pen. Here my son gave them a child's swimming pool to swim in. From there they went to the island and were fenced in under the huge old oak tree. Eugene, following his own plans, built a feeder for them that automatically releases their pellets, protecting them from predatory birds and keeping them clean and always readily at hand for feeding. He used the metal shell of a juke box and two large sewer pipes that are filled from the top.

The hybrid white Pekin ducks are very beautiful and almost as large as the African geese. The geese are especially friendly. We can pick them up, pat them, and carry them around. They remain very calm, apparently liking the attention. A little brown duck somehow got into our shipment and they told me that one was mine. I named him (her?) Rudolf for my older brother, whom I loved very much. Tiny, pugnacious, he picks fights with the placid geese! They ignore him.

I learned something new about the ducks and geese and how they are of value to the pond. It seems that the egrets are attracted not only to the fish in the pond but also to the small snails that inhabit the shallow

A Perfect Evening

In late June we had barbecued hamburgers around 7 o'clock and then we all went down to the point. I had saved a big bag of onion tops. Eugene fed the fish and then he pulled in the fish trap so he could count, measure, and release. We do this from time to time to check. The catfish were a good size, lively and healthy.

Our curious and friendly birds came up out of the water and started milling around us, apparently hoping. Their hopes were rewarded as we began handing out onion tops. All the geese and three of the hybrid ducks ate them from our hands. The smaller Swedish Blue seemed a little timid.

I especially enjoyed feeding the big geese, as they would daintily retrieve a morsel and constantly "talk" and ask for more, more, more. But when we stopped feeding, they showed no resentment or aggressiveness but simply wandered off and went back to swimming. All, that is, except the big gander who took a parting shot by untying my shoelaces!

It didn't get really dark then in the evening until nearly 9 o'clock so we sat around for a couple of hours just watching and listening to the crickets and tree frogs and, occasionally, the distant hoot of an owl.

Altogether, for us, it was a perfect end to a perfect day.

water. As soon as the ducks and geese were released, they began fishing for the snails but stayed close to the island. By performing this service, they keep the snails pretty well under control, and the pond is less attractive to the egrets. Everything seems to have its uses — we keep learning more all the time. It's beginning to sound a lot like companion planting, isn't it? An aquaculture version of *Carrots Love Tomatoes*.

The tiny snails that live in the mud at the edge of the pond are nutritious. They, like the bullfrogs, apparently appear spontaneously when conditions are environmentally right.

Wild Ducks and Geese Visit Our Pond

We like the white Pekin ducks and I sometimes think our family's preference for "white" is our subconscious ancestral genes kicking up. The centuries-old Riotte crest is a swan on a field of azure, surmounted by the usual crown and mantling of such relics of the past. Swans, which once graced the ponds on our château in southern France, are beyond us, but something in our mental makeup gives us pleasure to see those white ducks swimming around. The white ducks are not in the least "class-conscious" and welcome them without question when wild ducks come down to join the flock.

They don't have the same noble attitude toward wild geese, however. They are not only very standoffish but they are also quite aggressive in defending their territory. But the Canada geese that came down a few days ago are much bigger, and, in spite of the ducks' annoyance, they stayed for three days before resuming flight. I think we must be under one of their flightways; we often see and hear them in both spring and fall. Their V-shaped flight pattern is always led by a female goose — when she tires, another female takes her place. They fly rapidly, honking loud enough to wake us up at night, and have been known to fly as high as 29,000 feet above sea level. We think the wild geese are very

As I said, the ducks and geese, when released and the fence opened, went down to the water's edge and began walking around in the shallows, drinking and fishing for snails. What they did not do was *swim*. They remained on the island for nearly twenty-four hours. We could not understand this. The year before, when we released the ducks, they could not wait to get in the water and swim.

All of our family is very fond of spring green onions. Joan saved all the green onion tops and began taking them to the island and feeding them to the ducks and geese. They were avid for green stuff while fenced in.

Early the next morning after the birds were released but were still on the island, Joan went out in the boat and began throwing green onion tops in the water at some distance from the island. It was too much for the ducks and geese and they swam joyously out to get them and have been swimming ever since.

That, too, is a bit odd. Somehow we thought they would separate — ducks to ducks and geese to geese. Not so. They all swim together, as a body, quite companionably as if they were all the same species. And our older flock of ducks stay to themselves, cautiously watching the newcomers from a distance, very curious.

To people like us this is a very intriguing situation — what will they do next? We are simple folk, easily entertained, and it doesn't take much to make us happy!

Raising Ducks Sensibly

While our purpose in raising ducks was recreational, for the pure joy of having them swim around on our pond and watching their funny antics (they like us, too, and often come up and sit by our chairs when we are out on the lawn), there are a few basic rules for those who take ducks more seriously.

If you intend to have a breeding flock and winter them over, you must make advance preparations for a house or some other shelter. Keep in mind that you should provide at least 4 square feet of floor space per bird. The large, well-feathered breeds can stand cold but dislike drafts.

Ducks, as a rule, don't sleep much at night, so it's best to shut up the shelter completely. Instinctively nervous to begin with, they are even more so during the night hours, when they cannot see a potential enemy. Close them in, but in warm weather provide shutters or screened windows for proper ventilation.

Some breeds may need special winter care in the North, but most ducks will winter over well in a good shelter. In the South, make sure that plenty of water is always available, shade is provided for midday, and the night shelter is well ventilated.

North or South, make the duck house as predator- and rodent-proof as possible. Rats have been known to clean out a season's hatch of ducklings in a single night. If you live in the country, you also have to fear raccoons and skunks, as well as weasels and ferrets, which will kill ducks of all ages.

With this in mind, make the foundation, bottom boards, door, and windows of the duck house as sound as possible. When you fence your yard, bury a good foot of the poultry netting or wire fencing about 6 inches deep and angle it out from the pen. This effectively stops animals from digging in. Ducks kept in a small space should also have netting over the top of the outside run; this will stop the occasional bird who has a notion to fly out. It will also keep wild birds from flying in to share the ducks' feed.

Sanitation

Ducks are by their very nature messy creatures. For one thing, they need to splash their heads around. As I found out to my dismay, their frequent droppings are great watery splashes, so it is difficult to keep them in housing suitable for chickens. But if you want to keep ducks, there are several ways to overcome the watery problem in a restricted space. Plan on a pond or plenty of grazing land if you intend to keep a large flock. For summer in the North and in warm southern climates, the best foundation for both a fenced run and a shelter is a layer 6 inches to a foot deep of well-drained pea gravel, in conjunction with a high-pressure hose. Washing with a stream of water daily will force the mess down into the gravel. Add to this procedure a weekly raking to get up the loose feathers and accumulated leaves and sticks.

Water for Ducks

For us, of course, water for swimming and drinking presents no problem. For ducks who do not have such facilities handy, a length of metal storm gutter, sometimes obtainable at salvage yards, may be used. There are, of course, various types of waterers that you can purchase. As previously mentioned, ducks like to wet their heads — easily accomplished in a pond situation, but a little more complicated when using a storm gutter. If they can't submerge their entire heads, they soon will learn to dip quickly in one side and then the other. Such a watering arrangement is deep and wide enough so they can get their whole bills in to drink.

On a warm day, when ducks do a lot of drinking, you can keep a steady supply of water by running a length of hose to the trough and reducing the flow to a small trickle. In winter a bucket of water given daily will usually be sufficient. Generally by then the flock has been reduced to just a few breeders.

Feeding Your Ducks

Our ducks get a large part of their food from the pond — we planted arrowhead, pickerel weed, and wapato tubers specifically for their benefit (see *Sources*). Ducks eat marsh and water plants, including pond weeds, grasses, sedges, and rushes. They also eat floating plants and water animals that they can pry out of the water or mud. Freshwater diving ducks eat plants and dive to the bottom for roots, seeds, snails, and newly hatched insects. In fresh water, these divers eat insects, young beetles, bugs, dragonflies, mayflies, stone flies, and caddis flies.

Ducks, fed on the farm, can receive the same dry food as the layer mash given to the chickens if they are being overwintered. Grind together field corn, buckwheat, and other small grains, using cob and even husk for beneficial roughage. To increase protein, give them table scraps, bone meal, leftover meat, fish meal, and fat scraps, as well as fruits, vegetables, nuts, and seeds. Chop up the feed, as ducks' bills aren't designed for pecking. Cracked corn is usually less expensive than any prepared poultry mash or pellets. Some feed companies mix special waterfowl formulas. Garden residue such as carrot tops and other greens are welcomed, along with table scraps and peelings.

Ducks that do not dive for their food are called *dabbling* ducks. Wood ducks eat marsh plant fruits, and many nuts and fruits of water lilies. Domestic ducks almost all developed originally from wild mallards. White Pekin ducks, which weigh about 8 pounds, are the most common commercially raised ducks in the United States. Duck farming near metropolitan areas — on Long Island, New York, for example — can be a profitable business.

Raising Ducklings

Buying a batch of day-old ducks as we did is the easiest way to begin. Often a feed store will carry them, or you may purchase some from a hatchery or by mail. One of our friends who owns a ranch has a small incubator and hatches his own ducklings from eggs laid by his flock. Feed stores sell incubators (if you plan on incubating duck eggs, make sure yours has holders large enough), or buy from a catalog. Our friend sets up his incubator before the eggs arrive. He fills the water pan and puts a small piece of sponge in so that it protrudes a couple of inches (this is because waterfowl eggs need more humidity than do chicken eggs). Then he sets the temperature control at 95°F. It is then checked carefully with a fever thermometer. The exact temperatures recommended are 99 to 100°F for a forced-air machine and 101 to 102°F for a still-air machine.

Do not wash the eggs even though they may be dirty. This is because the mother duck puts on a coating that keeps out bacteria and helps keep internal conditions right. Flick off any dry soil with a thumbnail. Put the eggs in the incubator, keeping water and sponge well supplied. Turn eggs twice a day and spray at each turning with lightly warmed water. Turnings should be discontinued on the 25th day, but continue sprinkling water when the eggs start to pip.

The ducklings will begin pipping four weeks to the day from the start of incubation. Dip the eggs in warm water once the first little egg tooth appears, to facilitate hatching. From there on, it is best to let nature take her course.

Leave the young ducklings in the incubator until each is fully dry and actively walking around. Then one by one, as ready, place them in the brooder — a good-sized box sufficient to provide a square foot of floor space for each duckling. An infrared brooder bulb, encased in a metal hood, over the middle, providing warmth.

Place absorbent litter, layered several inches thick, on the bottom. Sand, if stirred frequently, is good, as are crushed corncobs. Shredded leaves, bagged in the fall, are cheap and will work well with a daily

Mother Duck

If your ducks are allowed the freedom of a large area, as ours are, one day a mother duck may surprise you. The female makes a nest, usually in a clump of grass, a hollow, or a hole in a tree. She lays from 5 to 12 eggs. After the female starts to sit on her eggs, the drake wanders off by himself. The ducklings hatch from three weeks to a month later.

Most ducklings can run, swim, and find food by themselves on the day they hatch. They grow quickly and have most of their feathers in about a month. They learn to fly in five to eight weeks. A mother duck keeps her young together so she can protect them from other birds and animals. But sometimes when one female with ducklings meets another, some of her young shift to the other mother! The more a duck quacks and swims around the ducklings, the more youngsters she attracts to her. Some females end up with twenty to forty ducklings, and others have only two or three.

stirring. Change the litter frequently — even the smallest ducks will splatter their food and water all around, and it is important that the young ducks be kept dry and unchilled until they are well fledged and have their waterproof feathers.

Provide coarse, crumbled feed several times a day: Give them all they seem to want. Include in the brooder a shallow water pan with a rock in the center. Move it often, making sure each time that the litter under the pan is well stirred and dry. Move the water pan each time you refill it.

On the third day, raise the brooder light so the floor temperature is 90°F. Watch the birds: If it is too warm, they'll run off to the corners of the box; if too cold, they'll cluster under the lamp. Keep the temperature at 90°F until the 11th or 12th day, then lower it to 80°F. By this time they will begin sprouting feathers. Ducks grow fast, as I found out, and by three weeks, if well fed, they'll weigh about 3 pounds. And, of course, they'll need more space, so put them in a pen with the brooder at 75°F. At four weeks you can turn it off. If temperatures are moderate, the ducks can be put out into the grass.

Feeding Young Ducks

Maximum growth is encouraged when the ducks are fed a diet that provides 20 to 22 percent protein for the first two weeks and 16 to 18 percent from two weeks to twelve. Commercial feed mixtures are available specifically for ducks and geese. But you can use chick starter if specialized food is not available.

According to John M. Vivian *(Raising Ducks & Geese)*, it is advisable, for the first several weeks, to feed small-pelleted ³⁄₃₂-inch or coarse-crumbled feed. From then on, larger pellets (³⁄₁₆ inch) will give good results. Ducklings choke on fine, powdery mash if it's dry, and up to 25 percent of the feed may be wasted. During the first two weeks, give the ducklings all the feed they want; after that, limit them to two or three feedings a day. After a month, give them one meal in the evening and encourage them to forage in a succulent pasture throughout the day. Grit, which encourages digestion, should always be accessible.

Geese Are Quite Wonderful

No question about it: Geese are very intelligent — but they can also be very aggressive, some breeds more so than others. I have several times heard the story of their being used in Scotland to protect the whiskey distilleries both by their aggressiveness toward strangers and by the warning they give of an outsider's presence by their loud cackling.

And then there is the story recorded in early Roman history of how the sacred geese in the temple of Juno saved the city. In 390 B.C., the Gauls, a fierce northern people, attacked the Romans. The invaders drove the Romans to a steep rocky hill known as the Capitol, which was used as a fort. One night, the consul Manlius was awakened by the cackling of the guard geese. Rushing to the wall, he saw that the Gauls had almost climbed it. His shouts and the noise of the geese woke the other Romans, and they defeated the Gauls.

At the right time and place, that characteristic of aggressiveness is just fine, but I am not crazy about geese in a small poultry yard. A number of years ago we raised a half-dozen geese and penned them in the yard with the chickens. They were large, healthy, and unfriendly. When the children went out to gather the eggs, the geese delighted in nipping them from the rear. The kids were scared of them, so I went out and gathered the eggs. Before long, they were switch-hitting me the same way. I told my husband, "Those geese have got to go!" And "go" they did: The first provided us with delicious roast goose for Thanksgiving dinner; the second was the main meal at our Christmas celebration; and the rest went into the freezer. I can understand the English tradition of roast goose for Christmas, for few birds are tastier. And if you do dress out a goose, be sure to save the down, for it makes lovely pillows.

The geese we raised were the White Embden, which grow bigger than the Toulouse, 35 pounds or so. They are a popular breed and if you buy geese, goslings, or eggs from a local farm, that is what you will probably get. The goslings cost several dollars each.

The goose's neck is a little longer than that of a duck and not so gracefully curved as a swan's. African geese have unusually long necks. Geese are good swimmers. They can walk on land better than can either swans or ducks because their legs are longer and nearer the middle of their bodies. Heavy layers of down (the valued goose down for pillows and comforters) underlie their dense plumage. Geese rub their feathers with an oil produced by a gland near their tails. This oil waterproofs their bodies.

Geese have long lives and sometimes reach more than 30 years of age in captivity. The wild Canada geese pair off and mate for life. Re-mating by a goose or gander whose partner has died is rare. We have noticed that when wild geese visit our pond, there are always two of them. We like to welcome them even if the ducks don't. But we keep a respectful distance.

Feeding Geese

Geese, both wild and tame, usually eat grains and vegetables, and sometimes insects and small water creatures. Penned geese should have a daily grain ration, but give them just a moderate amount until time for slaughter. Geese make great weeders, especially in the corn patch after the crop is well up. Let the geese fatten early and they will slow down on their job of weeding. Like ducks, they are happiest when allowed to graze, but can be enticed with a little grain to bring them into their shelter in the evening. Be sure to provide shelter in winter.

Geese are much less waterbound than are ducks, not needing to splash around nearly as much. Often wild flocks of Canada geese will feed avidly in mowed or cutover grainfields, swooping down on them during their annual migration. Geese can make do with various kinds of food. If they are kept penned, clean, fresh water must be available at all times.

Caring for Goslings

I have always loved the word "gosling"; it sounds light and fluffy like goose down itself, dainty and airy. But there is nothing delicate about goslings themselves. Scrounge around and find a discarded auto tire. Fill it with straw, and then persuade a goose to accept it. She will lay her eggs, raise her young (her husband helps), and defend them with all the viciousness of a mother grizzly. As previously mentioned, beware. A big goose, wings out, neck stretched almost ramrod straight, hissing like a steam engine, means business, and no mistake. That beak can break a grown man's arm, so keep kids and dogs out of the pen if there is a mother goose nesting.

But geese aren't all bad. Lots of farm children like to make pets of them, and they are good pets because they are so intelligent and trainable. I think they are better natured when allowed free roam. They will join you for a walk in the woods, talk to you, and will try to pick grain out of your back pocket. Just be cautious until the goose/gander knows who's boss. But if they are defending their nests or young, take extra care in dealing with them.

Incubating Geese

It is just possible that you may develop a real liking for geese after you get to know them better and decide you would like to incubate and brood them. Follow the same procedure as with ducks, but soak each egg in warm water for about the count of 10 at each twice-a-day turning. It takes about 30 days for the larger breeds to hatch — a few days less for the smaller Chinas. Waterfowl eggs, such as ducks and geese, can be held for up to a week before incubating. They should be turned twice daily, sprayed daily, and stored at a moderate temperature, neither too hot nor too cold (about 60°F).

Keeping Them Clean

Compared to duck droppings, those of geese aren't nearly so repulsive, but they're bigger! Overwintering geese can be a problem unless you have a big barnyard. If you have a reasonably large area for free range, they might just select a place of their own for overwintering and solve the problem.

Slaughtering

On the other hand, fall might just be a good time to decide to slaughter them, as we did. Dress them out just as you would a duck, cutting

Aquatic Plants for Waterfowl

You can obtain seeds and tubers to plant around the perimeter of the pond for waterfowl food, as ground cover, and to aid in erosion control. We chose fast-growing Japanese millet or duck millet, an annual that produces an abundance of seed enjoyed by waterfowl and upland game birds. It does best in damp to muddy soils and should be planted 25 to 40 pounds per acre. German millet prefers moist soils and is good for waterfowl when flooded. Sesbania seed or swamp pea is a favorite food for waterfowl, game birds, and mammals.

Sago pondweed tuber (*Potamogeton pectinatus*), a perennial, is one of the best wild duck foods, eagerly eaten by waterfowl for its seeds as well as tubers. It will tolerate brackish water. Wild celery plants (*Vallisneria americana Michx*) have tubers and seeds excellent for ducks and are some of the best plants for fish.

Arrowhead, or wapato duck potato (*Sagittaria latifolia*), should be planted in water 1 to 18 inches deep and will withstand periods of drought or flooding. Waterfowl like it. Bulrush (*Scirpus acutus*), a perennial, is good for cover, food, and erosion control.

False bittersweet vines (*Solanum dulcamara*), a perennial, has berries that cling to the vines long into the winter. Waterfowl love it.

Proso millet shows good drought resistance and has large seeds attractive to game birds and songbirds. An annual, it should be planted 15 to 20 pounds per acre.

Duck wheat, an annual, is a fast-growing plant, producing abundant seeds and continuing to frost. It is a good seeder. Plant 20 to 30 pounds of seed per acre.

For a perennial ground cover, my son chose switchgrass, a bunch grass that provides excellent spring nesting areas and cover in the winter. It grows 2 to 5 feet tall in low, moist areas and will withstand flooding. It is good for erosion control. Plant 10 to 12 pounds of seed per acre.

Another choice is reed canary grass seed, a perennial that provides food and good cover for winter survival and spring nesting for waterfowl and upland birds. Very good for erosion control, it grows 3 to 6 feet tall. Plant 10 to 12 pounds of seed per acre.

out the vent, and then making a cut from vent to keel. Put your hand in and work along the keel, pulling the viscera out. You'll need to open the neck cavity as well, probably splitting the neck skin after head and neck are chopped off. Make sure all the tubes are out.

The lungs may be difficult to remove. In a split bird they are obvious, noticeably pink and lying under thin membrane up along each side of the breastbone. You'll need to dig for them if you are dressing your bird whole — get every bit out. Remove the oil gland, feet, and all — and prepare for an unusual treat.

Breeds of Geese

The hatchery we order from offers White Embden and Gray Toulouse; they're in the most demand. Both are noted for their extremely fine meat quality. The White Emden is 100 percent white feathered, as its name implies. Gray Toulouse are sometimes referred to as the Gray Goose. You can expect both to be in the 14- to 18-pound range by Christmas when placed during the spring months.

The hatchery also has the White Chinese, which is a smaller goose in the 13-pound range, and the graceful African. The Africans are much larger than the White Chinese and, we think, are the most beautiful geese. This spring (1996) my son looked at their picture and couldn't resist them — so he ordered a half dozen along with 12 more ducks. We plan to raise geese and ducks together, and hope they will get along, and maybe — just maybe — the geese will help to protect the ducks from predators, which arrive in daytime as well as after dark. The attractive African ducks are white with dark wings. A dark streak extends from the head down the back of the neck.

This hatchery also offers Weeder goslings, an assortment of two or three different breeds, which can be had for a comparatively low price. The minimum order for all goslings is 10, and you can mix to your own preference if you wish.

Chapter 10

FROGGING FOR
FAMILY FUN

Early on I suspected that I was allowed to go frogging with my dad and the boys because they needed someone to hold the lantern — that left everybody else free to hunt. I didn't mind. I was a little small for my age and a bit on the skinny side, so I wasn't all that great at using the frog spear anyway. And turning a small put-down into a small triumph was a victory for me — one I savored, for it gave me my own status and admitted me to full partnership with my dad and my brothers, Josef, Anton, Emil, and Rudolf.

I was good at what I did. I've always had sharp eyesight, and even today, at 88, I have 20/20 vision. I could spot and warn of the water moccasins before anyone else saw them — everybody being so busy concentrating on hunting. The water moccasin is a semiaquatic pit viper (*Agkistrodon piscivorus*) of the southern United States, closely related to the copperhead. It is sometimes called "cottonmouth moccasin." I'm proud to say no one was ever bitten.

There are about 2,000 kinds of frogs living today. The giant frog of West Africa, growing about a foot long and weighing as much as a fox terrier when fully grown, is the largest frog known.

Frog hunting at night in some ponds can be very dangerous. Of course we avoided heavily infested ponds, but sometimes the snakes were found unexpectedly in ponds formerly free of them. Like the frogs, they too hunted. They tended to migrate from pond to pond. Now, we kill the snakes if any get into our catfish ponds and rarely have a problem. And since frogs have few natural enemies, they tend to increase with this protection.

The catch phrase "Build it and they will come" has been sadly overworked but I can't resist using it again. Frogs love to go "hop-about" and find ponds irresistible, much to our delight because we welcome them. We even love the nighttime serenade — that raucous bellow reminiscent of a bull. And that occasional splash is music to our ears as we sit out on the patio.

Having grown up with a fishing, hunting, and frogging family, I guess it was just natural that I should be attracted to a man who liked to do those things as well. We had hunted and fished together, but when he admitted to a liking for frogging also, I knew I had found my prince.

So we married and reared kids of our own. As they grew up they, too, became interested in camping and outdoor sports. My aim hadn't improved much with the passing of the years, so again I held the lantern while those more adept at spearing filled the bags.

Maybe by now you are wondering how we kept out of jail with all that nighttime activity. Well, it so happened that at the time I was the secretary of Wirt Franklin, founder and first president of the Independent Oil Producers' Association. Mr. Franklin was a leader and a great man, but I remember him most because of his kindness to me and my family, particularly to my children. He had a large cattle ranch and he gave us permission to fish and hunt frogs in and on the many ponds on his property.

We were always *very* careful to close gates properly, whether fishing in the daytime or frogging at night. This will get you high marks if you are lucky enough to have permission to use private property. And I do strongly advise that you do get permission if you value your skin. Farmers and ranchers do not take kindly to unannounced visitors.

The Common Bullfrog

Most of you will know what the common bullfrog (*Rana catesbeiana* Shaw) looks like but for the benefit of those new to the sport, here is what I learned from Mary Dickerson's *The Frog Book*.

This bullfrog is a big one, both male and female often reaching a length of 7 to 8 inches. Like many creatures, they vary somewhat in color according to area, climate, and habitat. In general, they are green or greenish brown and may be of a light or dark shade. Most adult frogs such as the bullfrog have no tails.

Spots, if present, may be distinct or connected. Arms and legs are spotted or barred with dark. The underparts are white, distinctly or obscurely spotted and mottled with dark. The throat of the male may be yellow. The eyes are truly beautiful and may be either golden or reddish bronze. They look like glass in reflected light. The frog can close its eyes by means of a thin piece of flesh or membrane attached to the lower eyelid.

The head is broad and flat, the body stout and flat. The ear of the male is much larger than the eye but the ear of the female is about the size of the eye and the lateral folds are not present. A strong fold of skin extends from behind the eye to the arm, curving around the ear. The toes are broadly webbed; the only free joint is the last joint of the fourth toe. The shorter front legs prop the frog up when it sits on the ground, and break its fall when it jumps.

In general they range in North America, east of the Rocky Mountains including Florida and Texas. Bullfrogs are also found in Canada.

Habitat

Bullfrogs are usually late in coming permanently from their hibernation. In the North it is often late May or early June (but in the South much earlier) before we take note of their deep bass voices coming from the ponds or become aware of their gigantic green bodies perched on partially immersed logs or floating among surface waterweeds. Their preference is for large ponds or lakes where deep water as well as shallow may be found, and they are screened from the shore by low willows, alders, or other water-loving plants. But small ponds also attract them.

Such places appeal also because of the sheltering growth of pickerelweed, arrowhead, and waterlilies, which make good hiding places. And under the leaves and stems and about the roots are to be found crawfish; water beetles; a variety of bugs, snails, and shrimps; the larvae of dragonflies and mayflies — in fact, all sorts of delicacies for a water frog's menu. In this characteristic, the bullfrog is different from leopard and pickerel frogs. It does not hunt in any place other than the body of water in which it makes its home. We are not likely to find bullfrogs on a country stroll across meadows and through orchards even though the meadows and orchards may be near ponds or lakes.

We are more likely to see them if we go rowing on a river or pond; however, we have not found this to be entirely true. In our area, we have neighbors who have ponds fairly close to ours and at certain times of the year, perhaps due to overcrowding, bullfrogs do migrate from one pond to another, possibly seeking more or a greater variety of food, or less competition. They proceed by successive leaps, about 3 feet each in length. A bullfrog can cover a distance of 5 or 6 feet without difficulty, notwithstanding his large, heavy body. Many frogs can jump twenty times their own length, on level ground. A wet bullfrog leaping across a dry surface leaves curious tracks, interesting in that they show how large a part of the under portion of the body and thighs strikes the ground forcibly after each leap, and how the frog "toes in" with its front feet. I find their hopping quite graceful and love to watch them.

Frogs help humans by eating insects. They are often sold to schools where students use them to study anatomy. Fishermen use them as bait. Bullfrogs are considered good pets when they have a proper place to live. Like good farmers everywhere, we kill only a limited number for food, making certain that a sufficient number of the larger frogs are left for breeding.

Color varies greatly, not only by sex but also among individuals of the same sex. The bullfrog has considerable control over his color. In warm air, exposed to bright light, his skin may become a beautiful spotless yellow-green, very light in tone. But a frog just from the mud, or a place of concealment in deep water, may be so dark he is nearly black. Experiments have shown that light has much to do with these color changes; such modifications may take place with changes of light even when temperature and moisture conditions remain the same. In Oklahoma's bright sunshine, ours are mostly lightly spotted yellow-green.

The common bullfrog is a powerful swimmer, with great strength and length of hind legs (sometimes measuring 7 to 10 inches long), and very large webs. It is interesting to watch it dive. It straightens its legs, then slowly draws them forward into position for the second stroke. The huge web is alternately extended into a flat, resisting membrane and then folded again as he draws his leg forward. The eyes are shut; that is, they are flattened until level with the head, by being lowered in their sockets, which project downward from the roof of the mouth.

This takes the eyes out of danger during the swift motion through the water, but also necessitates the frog swimming rapidly but a short distance at a time. He must either stop or slacken speed, opening his eyes to see where he is. Then, if an enemy is near, he can make a new plunge, with eyes again lowered. Like the toad, the frog has no outer ear to hinder him in swimming. The eardrum is at the surface of the head, covered and protected only by the moist skin. But Mother Nature has given it adequate protection.

As the frog dives under water, something else takes place. Large air bubbles are given off by the nostrils, which are then closed tightly. He does not use his lungs while breathing under water, the nostrils being kept closed, and the throat showing none of the swallowing movements so noticeable when he is breathing air. The frog's moist skin is similar to a great gill stretched over the whole body. Consequently, the frog not only can live under the water for months at a time but also will, preferentially, spend a big portion of his time lying, with flattened body and closed nostrils, at the bottom of the pond.

When a frog is growing, it often changes its skin. It pulls its old skin off over its head ... and often eats it! Frogs may take a few years before they become mature enough to breed.

The Unsinkable Frog

Sometimes when a problem seems unsolvable, I think of the frog who fell into a pail of milk. Drowning seemed certain, but the frog refused to give up. He paddled around until he had made a pat of butter and, using it for a launching pad, jumped out!

The Voice of the Frog

We love their serenade. Frogs do most of their calling during the mating season. On a moonlit night in May or June, the deep-toned call of the frog seems particularly insistent — startling in the quiet. The bullfrog does not sing in chorus; his call is an isolated one. From the low pitch of his note, we think of him as the bass viol in the batrachian orchestra. The call resembles to a certain extent the roar of a distant bull but is more musical, with notes less blended and slurred. The pitch will vary with the individual.

If you'd like to imitate the call, try saying with a hoarse, deep-toned voice the syllables of its various interpretations — *be drowned, better go 'round, jug o' rum,* or *more rum.* Repeating in front of some reverberating hollow body gives a better imitation, as the words are slurred. The call has a more musical quality than we may realize. Some people say it sounds like a bass guitar being plucked underwater.

The frog also has another sound, not heard so often — a loud, high-pitched scream. This comes unexpectedly when he is seized by a huge enemy such as a hawk, an owl, or an otter.

Food for Frogs

The tongue of the frog is attached to the front part of its mouth and is sticky. Shooting it out quickly, it can capture insects and other animals. Bullfrogs feed upon insects and other small life of the pond — but this small green dragon also eats fish, small turtles, young water birds, and, regrettably, other frogs.

The frog has no conscience. If you put a large frog in your collecting pail with several smaller ones, you may find upon arriving home from the pond that several of the smallest frogs have disappeared, and feet and legs may be protruding from the capacious mouth of the big fellow. But the food chain is always present in the pond, just as it is elsewhere. If frogs prey upon other smaller frogs and fish, fish also prey upon the tadpoles. The delicately delicious legs of the frogs make them vulnerable to man — and they bring a good price per dozen at the markets.

Bug Zapper Gives Nature an Assist

Like many "great discoveries," this one came about by accident and intelligent observation. My son hung a bug zapper outdoors to repel mosquitoes and other flying insects so we could sit on the patio in peace. He noticed that frogs were coming up from the pond, located about 30 yards from the house, to congregate around the area outside of the low stone wall of the patio where the light from the zapper was apparent — and the electrocuted bugs were dropping, well, like flies. The frogs came in all sizes, some very large, and in great numbers.

Why? This question was soon answered. They were quietly huddled there enjoying a frog banquet — catching the insects as they dropped. The insects, though dead, were still moving through the air and therefore acceptable. And a frog's long, sticky tongue is incredibly quick.

We are a family of "tree worshipers" and the "point," like the island, was planned to save a particularly large, beautiful native oak. An electric cable, enclosed in a plastic pipe, leads to the point. We hung the bug zapper on a line stretching from the tree on the point to the tree on the island. It is positioned at the edge of the bank over deep water so both frogs and fish may benefit. A length of garden hose around the cable protects the trees.

The zapper has a pulley affixed to the top of it that rides on a ⅛-inch wire cable for convenience in bringing it in for maintenance and storage. The zapper operates on low-cost AC current. It has a photo cell that turns it on at dusk and off at daylight. For safety's sake, a ground fault breaker or receptacle to the current source should be installed. This is very important. A cord is also stretched from tree to tree from the bottom of the zapper to stabilize it in the wind. A second bug zapper has also been installed at the creek leading into the pond with the lines stretched between two large native pecan trees.

Fish also like to feed on flying insects, and will jump out of the water to catch them. This adds up to some free meals for them as well, giving them the food nature intended for their growth and health. Fish become accustomed to a feeding area. If you want some fresh catfish for supper, this might just be a good spot to wet your line.

(Courtesy of Eugene Achille Riotte)

Developing bullfrog tadpole. The right arm is shown breaking through the skin after the left one comes out of the breathing pore.

The absorption of the tail has started. Now the legs do all the work of swimming.

Tadpoles

Except at breeding time, the bullfrog is solitary in habit. And the breeding season is late, extending from the end of May into July. Bullfrog tadpoles do not develop into frogs during the first season, as do those of the leopard and pickerel frogs. It is usually the second season, sometimes even the third, before the transformation is made. Large bullfrog tadpoles may be found any month of the year, but it is usually during June and July that the final transformation is made. And so life in the pond goes on.

Chapter 11

THE SUCCULENT
CRAWFISH

SMALL BOYS LOVE to go "crawdadding" and my son and a friend of his were no exception. And they did not need to go very far. In the low-lying area I have described elsewhere, just north of one of our large supermarkets, where flash floods occasionally carry cars off the street, there exists a "wetland" in miniature. Heavily traveled Interstate-35 is on one side, and the low-lying street on the other. In between is a marshy place where cattails grow in large numbers.

The kids spent many a happy Saturday morning in their small semi-tropical paradise. Crawfish, crawdad, and crayfish are all different names for the same freshwater cousin of the lobster. Regardless of what they are called where you live, chances are good that some can be found nearby. Wherever land is naturally wet, or has been flooded by man, this creature is likely to thrive.

It takes a little looking to find them, since they spend most of their lives underwater or in burrows deep in the ground. In the South, shallow ponds and streams with lots of plants are good places to look. In the North, find them in the shallow areas around lakes and rivers.

Crawfish in vegetation with fish

Some day, when you turn over the leaf of a pond lily or a pickerel plant, you may find these little creatures clinging to the underside. How did they arrive?

Most likely they were brought in and dropped by waterfowl flying in from other areas, or by that same beautiful snowy egret who brought in some unwanted fish from another pond.

Cherish them. Natural areas suitable for crawfish are disappearing, largely because their value to man and wildlife is not understood. They are quite harmless.

More than any other factor, it is the taste of crawfish that has led to widespread interest. Most gourmets compare crawfish to lobster and some think they are much better. As demand for seafood has spread to new parts of the country, these crustaceans have become a high-priced luxury item. Europeans have long appreciated crawfish and, in fact, import millions of pounds of North American crawfish each year.

Crawfish are preferred by many fishermen for bait. A live crawfish, hooked through the tail and dangled near a weed bed, is just too much temptation for many game fish to resist.

Man also benefits from the use of crawfish as laboratory animals for biological and medical research, according to Marley Beem, an aquaculture specialist at Oklahoma State University. Their large nerve cells make them an ideal subject for study of the nervous system.

Crawfish have the reputation of eating anything that does not move away fast enough. Basically this is true, but their principal food is decomposing plant material. Decaying vegetation becomes coated with bacteria and other animal life, making a nutrient-rich meal. Thus, by feeding on vegetation, crawfish speed up the release of nutrients that make growth possible for new plants. Crawfish also provide food for many different plant predators. Birds, fish, otters, and raccoons are all eager consumers of crawfish, given the opportunity.

The Life and Times of Crawfish

Crawfish are invertebrates, meaning they have no backbone. They rely instead on a tough outer-body armor for support and predator protection. As they grow, this armor becomes tighter. Shedding is in order so they'll have room to grow — this process is called molting. Now with a soft body, the newly molted crawfish hides in a thick weed bed or space

Roman Crawdaddies

As long ago as the time of the Roman Empire, crawfish were held in high esteem, although as a rule in those days they were the food of the poorer classes. The slaves ate the crawfish just as they were caught, but the crawfish destined for the imperial table were first fattened in earthenware pots, designed for the purpose.

between rocks for protection from predators and other crawfish until their outer parts again are hardened. Other crawfish eat them at this period.

The hard structure that covers the body of the crawfish is called the exoskeleton. It serves to keep the soft tissues of the body from being injured. Segments, or sections, divide the body. The front part is rigid, but the back part, or abdomen, has movable segments. There are five legs on each side of the body. The two front legs are shaped into large sharp claws, or pincers, much like those of the lobster, and are used for capturing and holding prey. The four other pairs of legs are for walking. There are also structures used in swimming, called swimmerets, under the abdomen of the crawfish. The crawfish also has two long feelers, or antennae, and two shorter ones. The crawfish feeds on snails, small fish, tadpoles, and insects. It is more active at nightfall and at daybreak.

The crawfish can often escape from danger by using snapping motions of its abdomen to swim backward rapidly. It paddles with the leaflike growth on the end of its tail called a "tail fan."

The crawfish varies in color, from pink, orange, and brown, to greenish black and dark blue. The clear white crawfish is a blind animal that makes its home in underground rivers.

Few animals can live both on land and underwater for long periods, but the crawfish can. Just as fish do, crawfish draw water across their gills to get oxygen. Unlike most fish, however, if their water does not have sufficient oxygen, they can simply leave their pond and breathe the air directly. If the air is moist enough, crawfish can live for months out of water.

What happens when one crawfish encounters another? A fight is likely, for crawfish are aggressive. Like many other animals, crawfish establish a territory. Other crawfish entering this area will be attacked. The loser uses quick sweeps of its tail to propel itself backward. But sometimes it may be eaten; crawfish are cannibals when given the opportunity.

Crawfish lay eggs, but all similarity to other egg-laying animals stops there. The southern red swamp crawfish begins mating in early summer. The male's sperm is deposited into a receptacle on the female. It is held there until eggs are laid in the fall. At that time, the eggs come in contact with the stored sperm and are fertilized.

Red swamp females burrow as deep as 24 to 36 inches in summer. Chimneys of soil up to 5 inches tall are left at the opening of each burrow. And it was these telltale chimneys that the boys searched for when they went "crawdad digging." The eggs and newly hatched crawfish remain attached to the underside of the female. The female with the eggs is said to be "in berry" because the eggs resemble small berries. The burrow provides protection from its enemies and moisture for the eggs while they are developing. When ponds are flooded by fall rains, the female emerges, and the young swim off to begin lives of their own. The time required for newly hatched crawfish to grow to harvestable size varies with climate and species. In Louisiana, red swamp crawfish hatched in autumn usually mate in late summer and egg laying takes place in the spring. Again, after hatching, the young remain attached as the female continues to feed.

Your interest in crawfish hunting may go no further than reading about them here, or you may want to try making traps and harvesting some wild crawfish yourself. So far as I know, there are no laws against hunting for wild crawfish, but as with other sports, you should get permission of the landowner if you hunt on private land.

Many Species

The crawfish lives in and along rivers and streams of every continent except Antarctica and Africa. There are approximately 250 species native to North America. Most likely there are dozens of different crawfish species in your state. On the ranch of our friend there are seven different species; we have found four on our land. The tails of our largest species, reddish brown and about 4 inches long, taste much like shrimp when fried. Very good!

THE LONG AND THE SHORT OF TURTLES

JUST A FEW DAYS AGO my granddaughter, Laura Elizabeth, found a turtle wandering about near the pond. She is very kindhearted and picked up the turtle and put it into the water. Her daddy was not too happy about this. Like most pond owners and anglers, he views turtles as a threat to fish communities. Upon doing some research, I have found that such is not entirely the case. Turtles are primarily scavengers, feeding on dead or dying fish and other aquatic organisms. In this manner they help to keep the pond clean, more than cause harm, and should not be indiscriminately destroyed. But it is also true that they may create problems by stealing bait and even fish from stringers. And snapping turtles sometimes prey on small ducks that hatch around the pond.

The Life and Times of Turtles

The turtle's shell covers its short, broad body, above and below, and makes up much of the skeleton. Turtles are the only group of higher animals that have most of their bony parts on the outside. The top part of

Two potential pond problems: turtles and American lotus

the shell is called the *carapace*. It is really the backbone and ribs, joined into a solid mass by many bony plates. It is covered by a layer of horny shields. The bottom part, or *plastron,* is built around the breastbone and probably the belly. The carapace and plastron are joined so that there are openings for the turtle's head, legs, and tail.

Freshwater turtles are more active than are land turtles, which are usually slow and clumsy. No turtles have teeth, another feature that distinguishes them from most other groups of higher animals, but the jaws have horny edges that can cut hard substances, and some turtles can make painful cuts. Turtles eat animals as well as plants, and many kinds eat decayed flesh. Some turtles will not swallow unless their heads are below water.

Many kinds of turtles grow quite large. Loggerheads sometimes reach 500 pounds. Their dark red meat tastes like beef, and many of these turtles are sent to market.

All turtles hatch from eggs. The female green turtle leaves the sea and digs a nest on the beach, lays her eggs, and covers them with sand. The sun warms the eggs, which hatch usually in about two months. Once the eggs are hatched, the young turtle makes its dangerous way to the sea; many kinds of mammals and birds are waiting to kill and eat it before it gets there.

Turtle Soup, Anyone?

If the pond owner enjoys turtle soup, turtle stew, or fried turtle, having a few turtles may be an asset. First you must catch your turtle — and here is how to draw it out. Have ready a big canner kettle filled with boiling water. Decapitate the turtle and place in boiling water for about 1 minute, depending on the turtle's size; use the tail as a handle to drop it in. Have sharp knives ready.

Remove and place onto a paper-covered outdoor table. Sever the skin close to the back shell and lift the back shell off. Turn the turtle over and

Reptiles with Shells

Turtles are actually cold-blooded reptiles with shells. They have lungs and breathe air, and they lay eggs with leathery or hard shells on land. *Freshwater turtles*, the most common type of turtle, live in freshwater ponds, rivers, and marshes. They have webbed feet and flatter shells than land turtles do.

Terrapins are water turtles that spend some of their time on land.

Land turtles or *tortoises* have thick legs and dome-shaped shells.

remove the lower plate in the same manner. (Both shells are easily removed after immersion in boiling water.)

With a sharp, pointed knife, next cut the soft belly flesh midline and remove the entrails just as you would clean a fish. Then, making four slits from the incision down the inside of each leg, cut away the skin. Peel the coarse outer skin from the body and cut it from the meat, along with the neck, tail, and feet. (The turtle skin peels almost as easily as does a banana.) Expose the pale pink muscles of meat. There is very little blood. Depending on its size, the turtle may be cut into two to four pieces, wrapped, and refrigerated.

Cubing about 2 pounds of the meat, dredge it in flour, and brown. Cover with cold water, adding salt, pepper, a little minced onion, and catsup. Simmer for about an hour. Test with a fork for doneness or slice off a little piece.

Meanwhile, to make gravy, blend a tablespoon of browned flour into a paste (called a roux) with a tablespoon of margarine (or butter). Mix with the liquid in the pan, add a glass of sherry, and — very gradually — stir in the yolk of 1 egg. Bring to a boil and add a can of undiluted cream of mushroom soup. Simmer for about 3 minutes.

Spoon turtle meat onto a heated serving dish. Pour gravy over meat. Serve over rice and accompany with a tossed green salad.

Turtle meat may also be prepared by pan-frying just as you would chicken, frying for about 30 minutes on each side. Be prepared to slam on the skillet cover to keep the meat from jumping out of the pan, as frogs' legs sometimes do. There is an old saying: "Turtle meat lives until the sun goes down."

Aficionados claim snapping turtles contain seven kinds of meat, including white meat, to which most are partial. Some claim the dark leg muscles taste like clam and the brisket like lamb. To me, it all just tastes like turtle.

Turtle soup makes a hearty meal and you can try it several ways — either with tomatoes and vegetables or with milk, butter, and a little cayenne. If you clean out the pond and have a lot of turtles to dispose of, can the meat and make it into whatever recipe you like best later on.

Trapping Turtles

If turtles become too plentiful, you can remove them by trapping, after checking to determine if your state has any regulations. Construct an effective trap by attaching a hardware cloth or "chicken wire" bottom to a square, four-board wood frame. Nail a slanted board to the outside of the trap, leading to the top edge. This serves as a ramp on which the turtle can crawl out of the water and into the trap. Drive a metal rod horizontally through two of the frame boards. Pass the rod through another "teeter" board, which extends from the edge of the trap to near the middle. When the turtle crawls to the end of the board, his weight will tip it forward and he will fall into the trap. A tough piece of fresh beef or pork should be suspended in the middle of the trap for bait. To keep the turtle in the trap, drive 20 D nails into the frame, slanting upward, 4 inches apart, 2 inches above the water.

Recipes

Raising your own food used to be taken for granted, but nowadays it is something special. Yet it is increasingly valued as people worry about the purity of food that is transported over many days and thousands of miles. The fish, ducks, geese, frogs, turtles, and crawfish that you raise on your own pond will be the freshest possible and of excellent quality if you provide healthy conditions.

Fish Is a Perfect Food

Fish has high-protein, low-calorie nutritional value. It is not only a treat for the palate but also good for you ... truly a guilt-free food.

Fish cookery is easy if you will keep in mind one basic rule that pertains to every method: Measure the fish at its thickest part (keep a small washable ruler handy), then cook it ten minutes for every inch of thickness.

The biggest mistake made in preparing fish is overcooking. Give it only the briefest sojourn in the pan, using a minimum of fat and flavoring it delicately.

A Pondside Fish Fry

Southwesterners are a convivial lot and use practically any excuse to have a fish fry or a party. Fish fries on the bank of a pond or a stream afford a wonderful means of cooking and eating fish, freshly caught. There is no better eating than fish, cleaned and rolled in cornmeal, then fried over an open fire in a large kettle or frying pan of hot fat.

Menu
Freshly caught fried fish
Texhoma Hush Puppies
Succotash Southwestern
Tex-Mex Skillet Cornbread
Green salad

FRIED PERCH OR OTHER PAN-FISH

Clean, wash, and dry the fish. Lay them in a large flat dish, and dredge with cornmeal or flour. Have ready a frying pan of hot drippings; put in as many fish as the pan will hold without crowding, and fry to a light brown. Send up hot in a chafing dish.

The many varieties of pan-fish — bluegill, flounders, river bass, weakfish, whitefish, and so on — may be cooked in like manner. In serving, lay the head of each fish by the *tail of the one* next to it.

TEXHOMA HUSH PUPPIES

Serves approximately 12

No chapter on fish recipes can be complete without the time-honored combination of fish and the legendary hush puppies. From my book In Nature's Hands, *this is my favorite recipe. You can fry hush puppies in purified oil, but to be really authentic they should be fried in the same oil as the fish.*

2 cups cornmeal
2 Tbsp. flour
1 tsp. baking powder
1 tsp. salt
1 large egg, beaten
1 cup buttermilk
4 Tbsp. minced red onion
1 Tbsp. finely chopped jalapeño pepper

Blend together dry ingredients. Add egg, buttermilk, onion, and pepper. Mix well. Drop by tablespoons in deep fat, preferably in which fish has been fried, heated to 375°F. Fry over medium heat until golden brown (about 5 minutes), remove, and drain on paper towels. Serve piping hot. This recipe can be doubled.

SUCCOTASH SOUTHWESTERN

Serves 6

All the recipes I have ever seen for this call for lima beans, but we prefer to make ours with black-eyed peas.

2 cups fresh black-eyes
½ pound "chunk bacon," sliced
4 cups fresh corn, cut from cob
½ cup chopped onion
¼ cup chopped green pepper
3 Tbsp. margarine
1 tsp. salt
½ tsp. pepper

Cook peas with bacon in salted water to cover for about 15 minutes, or until both are almost tender. Add corn and remaining ingredients; stir well. Cook, uncovered, over low heat 8 to 10 minutes, stirring often, until corn and the other vegetables are done.

If you are planning a cookout, this dish can be prepared a day ahead and refrigerated. It warms well, as the flavors seem to blend overnight.

TEX-MEX SKILLET CORNBREAD

Serves 12

1 Tbsp. vegetable oil
1½ cups self-rising cornmeal
1 cup buttermilk
2 large eggs, beaten
3 Tbsp. vegetable oil
1 (8¾-ounce) can cream-style corn
1 clove garlic, minced
½ cup chopped green pepper
8 slices cooked bacon, crumbled
¼ cup chopped fresh jalapeño peppers
2 cups (8 ounces) shredded sharp Cheddar cheese

Oil a 10½-inch cast-iron skillet with 1 tablespoon oil. Place skillet in preheated 350°F oven for 10 minutes, or until very hot. (This gives the cornbread a delicate toasted crust.) Combine cornmeal, buttermilk, eggs, oil, corn, garlic, pepper, bacon, and jalapeño peppers. Stir well. Pour half the cornmeal mixture into the hot skillet. Sprinkle with 1 cup cheese. Top with remaining cornmeal mixture. Bake at 350°F for 45 minutes. Sprinkle with remaining 1 cup cheese; bake an additional 10 minutes.

FRIED BROOK TROUT

Brook trout are generally cooked in this way, and form a really delightful breakfast or supper dish. Clean, wash, and dry the fish, roll lightly in flour, and fry in butter or clarified drippings. Let the fat get hot, fry quickly to a delicate brown, and take up the instant they are done. Lay for an instant upon a hot, folded napkin, to absorb whatever grease may cling to their speckled sides; then range side by side in a heated dish, garnish, and send to the table. Use no seasoning except salt, and that only when the fish are fried in lard or unsalted drippings.

BAKED TROUT

Rub a 3½-pound trout with salt. Place in a baking pan, cover with 2½ cups cooked tomatoes, ¼ cup diced onion, and ½ cup diced celery. When trout is cooked, place on a hot platter and keep in a warm place while preparing sauce. Strain tomato mixture. Beat 1 egg yolk with ½ cup cream, tomato sauce, and ½ teaspoon Worcestershire sauce. Heat to boiling and cook 2 minutes.

BAKED TROUT FOR CAMPERS

Reserve the large fish for this overnight cooking. At night, clean fish and remove heads. Season inside and out with salt and pepper, roll separately in waxed paper, folding ends in, and wrap in thick, wet newspaper. Dig a trench for each fish just deep enough to allow one inch of earth on top. Bury bundles. Build the campfire over the trenches and leave until breakfast time.

TROUT, RARE AND DELICIOUS

The acceptance of roast beef served rare was widespread even before it was realized that undercooked meat is very superior nutritionally. It may come as a surprise to know that undercooked fish is also delicious. Try this way of preparing trout or any other fish of delicate flavor.

Turn the fish in stone-ground yellow cornmeal. Have ready a skillet that is hot. Add a little oil, put in the trout, and let the cornmeal brown very lightly; then turn, cut off the heat, and leave just barely long enough for the trout to heat through but not cook. Serve at once browned side up. The flesh will be moist, sweet, and delicious. Season with either salt or a little lemon to be squeezed on as desired.

An army wife states that after living in Japan, she could no longer stand to eat cooked fish! She said she liked ice cold fresh fish cut into strips and dipped into a sauce of grated raw turnip with Japanese soy sauce.

BAKED SALMON-TROUT

I love the old cookbooks, the authors' respect for good food, the care they bring to its preparation, their conversational style, and their evident pleasure in their culinary achievement. In particular, I treasure my 1884 cookbook Common Sense in the Household, A Manual of Housewifery, *by Marion Harland, and in this chapter I will share some recipes from it. It contains recipes not to be found elsewhere on various species of fish and game that were once more abundant than they are now. There were few, if any, game laws in the nineteenth century and many species were free for the taking.*

Marion especially prized many kinds of fish. Her recipe for Salmon-Trout (Rainbow) makes her careful preparation, dramatic presentation, and her epicurean delight in the finished product sound almost like a religious experience. But her comment in conclusion reveals her sense of humor, bidding us laugh with her!

Those who have eaten this prince of game fish in the Adirondacks, within an hour after he has left the lake, will agree with me that he never has such justice done him at any other time as when baked with cream.

Handle the beauty with gentle respect while cleaning, washing, and wiping him, and lay him at full length, still respectfully, in a baking pan, with just enough water to keep him from scorching. If large, score the back-bone with a sharp knife, taking care not to mar the comeliness of his red-spotted sides. Bake slowly, basting often with butter and water. By the time he is done — and he should be so well-looked after that his royal robe hardly shows a seam or rent, and the red spots are still distinctly visible — have ready in a saucepan a cup of cream — diluted with a *few* spoonfuls of hot water, lest it should clot in heating — in which have been stirred cautiously two tablespoonfuls of melted butter and a little chopped parsley. Heat this in a vessel set within another of boiling water, add the gravy from the dripping-pan, boil up once to thicken, and when the trout is laid — always respectfully — in a hot dish, pour the sauce around him as he lies in state. He will take kindly to the creamy bath, and your guests will take kindly to him. Garnish with a wreath of crimson nasturtium blooms and dainty sprigs of parsley, arranged by your own hands on the edge of the dish, and let no sharply spiced sauces come near him. They would but mar his native richness — the flavor he brought with him from the lake and wild-wood. Salt him lightly, should he need it, eat, and be happy.

Marion concludes the recipe by saying, "If the above savor of bathos rather than 'common sense,' my excuse is, I have lately eaten baked salmon-trout with cream gravy." Bless you, Marion, reading your recipe is almost as much fun as eating the delicious dish it produces.

It was a different day and a different time and all Ms. Harland's recipes for game or fish refer to the subject in the masculine gender.

An Elegant Smoker and Smoked Catfish

During more than 65 years of eyeing my bewhiskered friends appreciatively, as I endeavor to decide what method of cookery will best enhance their deliciousness, I have tried just about everything short of dipping them in chocolate. Then my son discovered smoked catfish.

This came about in rather a roundabout fashion. If you want to hunt deer in Oklahoma, the best way is to secure a deer lease — and the finest ones are considered so precious that rights to them are sometimes put in wills! My son has just such a one, along with a lifetime hunting and fishing license. The deer lease yields not only deer, which may be taken during bow-and-arrow season, flintlock season, and rifle season, but also an occasional wild pig. These pigs are a cross between escaped domestic varieties and our native javelinas. They make excellent eating.

Herbs to Accompany Fish

Dill

Tarragon

Basil

Marjoram

Fennel

Turmeric

Sometimes the lessee takes in a partner to share the cost and for safety reasons. It so happened last fall that Eugene's partner was transferred by his company to another area, and he offered his smoker for sale. This partner, a machinist by trade, had made the smoker for his own use, crafting it lovingly with only the very best materials. Eugene bought the very large smoker — big enough to hold several fresh picnic hams, turkeys, chickens, haunches of venison, and fish.

Creativity seems to be one of our family characteristics, and Eugene is an artist in metal. Making a small trailer for his new acquisition was an irresistible project and we all teased him about going into a frenzy of whimsy, but the result was just adorable (there is no other term I can think of that describes it so well). It is Victorian in decoration and even boasts a metal roof elevated on tall poles. He painted the trailer a muted black and just before Christmas his daughter, Laura Elizabeth, tied bows of green and red satin ribbon on every suitable area. Smoker and trailer look like something that belongs in a carnival, smoking fragrantly away somewhere between the Ferris wheel and the merry-go-round.

SMOKED CATFISH

Serves 6 to 8

In the spring, around Easter, our family went fishing on a friend's ranch and we were lucky in catching several beauties in one of the older ponds. We decided to smoke them, and here is the recipe we used.

7 pounds catfish
2 cups water
½ cup firmly packed brown sugar
¼ cup salt
2 Tbsp. Worcestershire sauce
¼ tsp. dried dillweed

Cut the catfish into 1½-inch-thick steaks (skin on) and place them in a large, shallow dish. Combine remaining ingredients and pour over fish. Cover. Marinate in refrigerator 1 to 4 hours, turning occasionally. Smoke approximately 1 hour or just until tender. The time varies with the size of the fish. Fish should never be overcooked, so keep testing.

FRIED CATFISH

Skin, clean, and remove the heads. Sprinkle with salt and lay aside for an hour or more. Have ready 2–3 eggs beaten to a froth and, in a flat dish, a quantity of powdered cracker. Dip the fish first in the egg, then in the cracker (cornmeal may be used instead of cracker), and fry quickly in hot lard or drippings (cooking oil may be used). Take up as quick as done. Serve with Hush Puppies (page 159).

CAJUN CATFISH

Serves 4 to 6

Cajun cookery seems to be ever increasing in popularity. My stockbroker, who is Cajun, gave me this recipe.

3–4 pounds cleaned
    catfish chunks
1 tsp. salt
1 tsp. freshly
    ground black
    pepper
1 red onion
½ cup green onion
1 bell pepper
½ cup celery
⅛ cup olive oil
4 Tbsp. flour
1 (14–16-ounce)
    can tomato sauce
1 Tbsp. minced
    fresh garlic
¼ tsp. cayenne
1½ cups cooked rice

Season the catfish with salt and pepper. Chop the red and green onions, pepper, and celery, and sauté them in olive oil. Sprinkle flour on top and stir lightly. Add tomato sauce and seasonings. Add fish, being careful to lay chunks so that each piece is coated with sauce. Do not stir after adding fish. Simmer about 15 minutes. Serve over rice. Garnish with additional chopped green onions.

Broiling Fish

Small- or medium-sized fish, up to two fingers thick, are most satisfactorily prepared by broiling at 140°F. Allow 15–18 minutes, depending upon thickness. By using this method, you can avoid the unpleasant odor sometimes associated with cooking fish.

STEWED CATFISH

Writing The Manual of Practical Housewifery *in 1884, Marion Harland never hesitated to say what she thought — and she had this to say about catfish:*

Skin, clean, and cut off the horribly homely heads. Sprinkle with salt, to remove any muddy taste they may have contracted from the flats or holes in which they fed, and let them lie in a cool place for about 1 hour. Then put them in a saucepan, cover with cold water, and stew very gently for about ½–¾ of an hour, according to their size. Add a chopped shallot or button-onion, a bunch of chopped parsley, a little pepper, a large tablespoonful of butter, a tablespoonful of flour mixed to a paste with cold water; boil once, take out the fish carefully, and lay in a deep dish. Boil the gravy again, and pour over the fish. Send to table in a covered dish.

A Barbecued Fish Feast

In the Southwest, just about everything that will lie still gets barbecued sooner or later, including rattlesnake. In the old days it was served up under the name of "prairie eel" — often eaten by travelers who had no idea what it was. Rattlesnake is surprisingly good and tastes much like chicken. When we cleaned out the snakes in the cement blocks when the new pond was built, there were several large rattlers, which we skinned and cut up to be barbecued along with our catfish.

Menu
Barbecued Catfish
Southwestern-style Baked Beans
Oklahoma State Fair Onions
Garlic bread
Iced "Sun Tea"

My son built his own barbecue, which he lines with heavy-duty aluminum foil, then likes to use a combination of high-quality hardwood charcoal and mesquite chips. This makes the hottest, longest-lasting fire.

We like our barbecued fish served with baked beans, onions, garlic bread, and iced tea. I got the idea for deep-fried onions recently at the Oklahoma State Fair. We grow our own onions — red, yellow, and white —

and set aside the softball-sized ones weighing between 1 and 2 pounds. After the onion is peeled, cut it with an onion slicer to form a "blossom." Bread the onion in a light coating of an Italian seasoning and deep-fry for 3 to 4 minutes. The final product looks more like a burnt orange mum than an onion. Serve with a chili sauce–sour cream dip.

Iced tea is our favorite beverage. I have a friend in California who imports a special blend of African tea and sends me a supply from time to time. Our Oklahoma sun, in summer, often goes over 100 degrees, sometimes for several days in a row — so I make "sun tea." I place one tea bag in a fruit jar, cover, and let the sun make the tea.

We grow the large, beautiful, purple-sheathed garlic, practically guaranteed to knock you down at five feet. We thick-slice a loaf of French bread. We make a mix of low-cholesterol margarine and freshly chopped garlic, butter one side of each slice, form the loaf back together again, wrap in heavy aluminum foil, and place over the hot coals in the barbecue. Until you try out this complete menu, you just haven't lived!

BARBECUED CATFISH OR RATTLESNAKE

Serves 8

This is our family's favorite recipe. Fillets should be about 4 ounces each.

8 catfish fillets
1 tsp. salt
¼ tsp. freshly ground black pepper
¼ tsp. paprika
8 slices bacon, divided
4 tsp. lemon juice

Rinse fillets thoroughly in cold water; pat dry and sprinkle with salt, pepper, and paprika. Set fillets aside. Rattler sections are also prepared this way.

Place 2 slices of the bacon on a large piece of heavy-duty aluminum foil; place a catfish fillet lengthwise on each bacon slice. Sprinkle ½ teaspoon lemon juice over each fillet. Fold foil edges over, and wrap securely. Makes 8 packages.

Grill packets over hot coals 10 minutes. Turn packets and grill an additional 10 minutes, or until fish flakes easily (or rattler steaks are tender) when tested with a fork.

SOUTHWESTERN-STYLE BAKED BEANS

Serves approximately 8

½ pound bacon, diced
½ cup chopped onion
¾ cup honey
4 tsp. dry mustard
1 tsp. salt
⅛ tsp. cayenne pepper
4 cups cooked and drained small white beans (or three 15-ounce cans)

In a skillet, sauté bacon and onion until onion is tender. Remove from heat. Stir in honey, mustard, salt, and cayenne. Layer half the beans in a 2-quart covered baking dish; spoon half the honey mixture over beans. Repeat layers. Cover and bake at 325°F for 1 hour, or until honey mixture is absorbed. Prepare this recipe in advance to allow flavors to develop, and then reheat before serving.

BAKED STUFFED BASS

This stuffing is enough for a 4- to 5-pound bass, with or without head and tail. Other fish suitable for baking: whitefish, lake trout, pike, carp, pickerel, and shad.

3 cups cracker crumbs
⅓ cup butter
¾ cup chopped celery
¼ cup finely chopped onion
2 Tbsp. lemon juice
2 tsp. minced parsley
¼ tsp. rosemary
½ tsp. salt
¼ tsp. pepper
¼ cup hot water
4–5 pounds fish
1 Tbsp. salt
Cooking oil

Measure crumbs into bowl. Heat butter in a skillet; add celery and onion. Cook slowly until onion is transparent, stirring occasionally. Add to crumbs with a mixture of lemon juice, parsley, rosemary, salt, and pepper. Add hot water and mix thoroughly.

Rinse body cavity of fish with cold water, drain, and pat dry with absorbent paper. Rub cavity with salt. Lightly pile stuffing into fish, and skewer or sew opening. Place in shallow baking pan lined with aluminum foil. Brush surface with oil or cover with thin slice of salt pork or bacon. Bake at 350°F until fish flakes easily, about 45 to 50 minutes.

FRIED BASS

Use the small fish for this purpose. Clean, wipe dry inside and out, dredge with flour, and season with salt. Fry in hot butter or drippings. The bass should be done to a delicate brown — not to a crisp. The fashion affected by some cooks of drying fried fish to a crust is simply abominable.

Fried bass are a most acceptable breakfast dish.

CATFISH CHOWDER

Skin, clean, and cut off the heads. Cut the fish into 2-inch long pieces, and put into a pot with some pork fat cut into shreds (1 pound of pork fat to 12 medium-sized fish), 2 chopped onions or 6 shallots, a bunch of sweet herbs, and pepper. The pork will salt it sufficiently. Stew slowly for ¾ of an hour. Then stir in 1 cup of milk, thickened with 1 tablespoon of flour. Remove 1 cup of the hot liquid and stir in, a little at a time, 2 well-beaten eggs. Return liquid to the pot, throw in 6 Boston or butter crackers, split in half; let all boil up once, and turn into a tureen. Pass sliced lemon or sliced cucumber pickles with it. Take out the backbones of the fish before serving.

HEARTY FISH & VEGETABLE CHOWDER

Serves 6 to 8

2 medium onions
3 Tbsp. butter
4 cups thinly sliced
   raw potatoes
6 cups water
1 (12-ounce) can
   corn
1 (6-ounce) can
   sliced mushrooms
2 pounds firm white
   fish, filleted
Salt and pepper
½ cup dry sherry

Thinly slice the onions, and cook them in butter until soft but not brown. Add potatoes and water; cook until potatoes are tender. Add corn and mushrooms (with liquid from can). Cut fish into 2-inch pieces; add. Cook slowly until fish flakes and is tender, about 10 to 12 minutes. Season to taste and stir in sherry. Serve at once.

Frogs, Crawfish, and Turtles

Preparing Frogs for the Table

This is not nearly as unsavory as you might think. Skinning a frog is a simple and not unpleasant task. After the throat is slit, hold the frog by one leg with the left hand and dip it into running water, then sever the leg by which the frog is held. The frog's weight holds the skin taut and outlines the big leg muscles, making the cutting easy. Lay the knife down. With your right hand, slip the leg skin backward from the meaty thigh section. Do not remove it entirely. This action is something like taking off a glove wrong-side-out. Place the cleaned leg on a board and, with the wrong-side-out skin still attached, cut off the front end.

It's that simple: Catch your bullfrog, slit, sever one leg, slip the skin back, and cut at the hock. Sever the second leg, slip the skin, and cut it away with the foot; only pink, clean meat remains. (Usually no part of the frog except the leg is skinned, and there is little blood or odor.)

When you go frog hunting, have ready a half-gallon container with a tight lid to receive the cleaned frogs' legs, and they will be ready for frying when you arrive home. Cleaning them on the pond or creek bank also saves a mess in the kitchen and will give you high marks with the cook.

Health Aspects

Frog meat is classified as seafood and a white meat. It is highly digestible, rich in protein, and low in fat and calories, with a very high biological value, according to Dr. Rui Donizete Teixira (*Aquaculture Magazine*, March/April 1993). Recently, research at important institutions has proved that frog meat is the only animal product 100 percent efficient for the treatment of allergic alimentary disturbances in children. In the United States, 40 percent of all frog meat is consumed in hospitals.

SAUTÉED FROGS' LEGS

Serves 2

The French are famous the world over for their fondness for frogs' legs. Here is one of their best recipes. Four pairs of frogs' legs weigh about 1½ pounds.

4 pair frogs' legs
Milk to cover
1½ tsp. Season-All or Bon Appetit
½ tsp. onion powder
¼ tsp. white pepper
1 tsp. chopped parsley
Flour for coating
1 egg (optional)
6 Tbsp. margarine (or butter)

Soak frogs' legs in milk 1 hour. Remove from milk and sprinkle with Season-All or Bon Appetit, onion powder, pepper, and parsley. Coat lightly with flour. (May be dipped in egg first, if desired.) Melt margarine; as soon as it sizzles, add frogs' legs and sauté 7 minutes on each side, or until golden brown. Remove to heated platter. Spoon butter or margarine from skillet over frogs' legs.

Variations:

Frogs' Legs Provençale. Prepare frogs' legs as above. Remove to heated platter. To margarine in skillet, add ½ teaspoon garlic powder (or 1 teaspoon finely chopped fresh garlic), 1 tablespoon lemon juice, and 1 teaspoon fresh (or dried) parsley flakes. Stir to mix well. Pour over frogs' legs.

Frogs' Legs Aux Fines Herbes. Prepare frogs' legs as in main recipe. Remove to heated platter. To margarine in skillet, add ¼ teaspoon tarragon leaves, ½ teaspoon parsley flakes, ½ teaspoon chives, ½ teaspoon dill seed, and 2 tablespoons dry white wine. Stir well and pour over frogs' legs.

Quickie. Season prepared frogs' legs with salt and pepper, dip into fine cracker or bread crumbs, then into slightly beaten egg, and again into crumbs. Let stand 15 to 20 minutes. Fry in hot, deep fat (375°F), 3 minutes or until browned. Serve plain or with tartar sauce.

CRAWFISH ÉTOUFÉE

Serves 4 or 5

6 Tbsp. butter
2 cups chopped onion
2 cloves minced garlic
¼ cup celery, chopped
1 pound or 2½ cups crawfish tail meat
1¼ tsp. salt
¼ tsp. black pepper
⅛ tsp. red pepper
2 Tbsp. green onion, chopped fine
2 Tbsp. minced parsley

Melt butter in skillet or pot. Sauté onions, garlic, and celery until onions are clear. Add ⅛ cup water and simmer, covered, until vegetables are tender. Add tail meat, salt, and black and red pepper. Cook 15 minutes. Add green onion and parsley and cook 5 minutes more. Serve over hot steamed rice.

How to Eat Crawfish

Traditionally, crawfish are eaten while standing around the table. Use the thumb and forefinger of one hand to hold the body, and the thumb and forefinger of the other hand to hold the tail, just where it attaches to the body. With a twist, separate the tail from the body. Connoisseurs suck some of the juices from the body before discarding it. Use the thumb and forefinger of each hand to hold the tail, two to three segments back from where it joined the body. Peel the outer covering away from the thick end. Pull and twist the exposed tail meat free of the remaining covering. Pop into your mouth.

TRADITIONAL CRAWFISH BOIL

Cover your tables with plastic. Two-inch-long crawfish are about the minimum size for good eating. You'll need a very large cooking pot, a large wire basket to fit inside the pot, and an outdoor propane cooker for this recipe. Use 1 gallon of water for every 2 pounds of crawfish.

4 pounds crawfish per hungry person
1 pound salt for every 5 gallons water
1 packet Crab and Shrimp Boil for every 10 pounds of crawfish
Red pepper (optional)
Lemons, halved (optional)
Onions (optional)
Corn on the cob, quartered
Potatoes, quartered

Place crawfish in wire basket, making sure they are all alive. Rinse under cold running water; set aside. Pour water into cooking pot so that it is no more than ¾ full. Add salt, Crab and Shrimp Boil packets, and other seasonings. Bring to a boil and cook for 20 minutes. Add as many crawfish as can be immersed, along with some corn and potatoes. Take care not to get splashed. Cook for 10 minutes more. Remove from heat and let sit 20 minutes to absorb seasoning. Remove wire basket from water and dump crawfish, corn, and potatoes onto plastic-covered table. Seasoned water can be reused to cook more crawfish for the same meal. Keep bringing water back to a boil.

DEEP-FRIED CRAWFISH TAILS

Serves 4 to 6

1 egg, beaten
¼ cup evaporated milk
½ tsp. prepared mustard
¾ tsp. salt
¼ tsp. black pepper
¼ tsp. garlic powder
1 cup flour
½ cup cornmeal
½ tsp. baking powder
1 pound cooked and peeled crawfish tail meat

Beat the egg in a bowl and add milk, mustard, salt, pepper, and garlic powder. Mix well. In another bowl, sift flour, cornmeal, and baking powder together and stir to blend.

Dip tails in egg-milk mixture. Drain, then dip individually in the cornmeal-flour mixture. After all are dipped, drop into deep hot fat in a deep-fryer and cook until golden brown. Drain on paper towels. Serve with catsup or tartar sauce.

Under "Air Fresheners and Deodorizers," Julia Percivall and Pixie Burger, writing in their book *Household Ecology,* give this hint for cooking fish: "Don't ask me why, but a piece of apple placed in the pan along with the fish does much to tone down the fishy smell.

"The smell of fish on your hands can easily be removed with lemon juice or a lemon half — even a left-over squeezed-out rind and pulp will serve as a deodorizer."

STEWED TURTLE

Marion Harland expressed her opinions on anything and everything, and her cookbook is as entertaining as a novel. What's more, her directions are clear and understandable. She had this to say about turtles:

Land-terrapins, it is hardly necessary to say, are uneatable, but the large turtle that frequents our mill-ponds and river can be converted into a relishable article of food.

Plunge the turtle into a pot of boiling water, and let him lie there five minutes. You can then skin the underpart easily, and pull off the horny part of the feet. Lay him for ten minutes in *cold* salt and water; then put into more hot water — salted, but not too much. Boil until tender. The time will depend upon the size and age. Take him out, drain, and wipe dry; loosen the shell carefully, not to break the flesh; cut open also with care, lest you touch the gall-bag with the knife. Remove this with the entrails and sand-bag. Cut up all the rest of the animal into small bits, season with pepper, salt, a chopped onion, sweet herbs, and a teaspoonful of some spiced sauce (use your favorite), or a tablespoonful of catsup — walnut or mushroom. Save the juice that runs from the meat, and put all together into a saucepan with a closely fitting top.

Stew gently for fifteen minutes, stirring occasionally, and add a great spoonful of butter, a tablespoonful of browned flour wet in cold water, a glass of brown sherry, and lastly, the beaten yolk of an egg, mixed with a little of the hot liquor, that it may not curdle. Boil up once, and turn into a covered dish. Send around green pickles and delicate slices of dry toast with this dish.

SOURCES

Books

Bayramian, Mary. *Cooking Around the World, Chicken and Fish*. San Francisco: Troubadour Press, 1977.

Bennett, G.W. *Management of Lakes and Ponds*. New York: Van Nostrand Reinhold Co.

Bernath, Stefen. *Common Weeds, Tropical Fish*. New York: Dover Publications, 1978.

Calkins, Carroll. *Gardening with Water, Plantings, and Stone*. Walker Publishing, 1974.

Chalmers, Irene, with Milton Glaser and friends. *Great American Food Almanac*, New York: Harper & Row.

Coventry, Ralph. *Exotic Butterflies & Moths*. Laguna Beach, CA: Walter T. Foster Publishing Co., 1971.

Cunningham, Marion. *The Fannie Farmer Cookbook*. New York: Bantam Books, 1995.

Dickerson, Mary C. *The Frog Book*. New York: Dover Publications, Inc.

Dodge, Natt N. *Flowers of the Southwest Deserts*. Globe, AZ: Parks & Monuments Assn., 1976.

Firth, Grace. *A Natural Year*. New York: Simon & Schuster, 1972.

Ghosn, M.T. *Origin of Birthstones and Stone Legends*. Inglewood Lapidary, P.O. Box 701, Lomita, CA 90717, n.d.

Harland, Marion. *A Manual of Practical Housewifery*. New York: Charles Scribner's Sons, 1884.

Harris, Ben Charles. *Eat The Weeds*. Barre, MA: Barre Publishing, 1975.

Harris, Lloyd J. *The Book of Garlic, Folklore & Medical Data*. Berkeley, CA: Aris Books.

Hart, Rhonda Massingham. *Bugs, Slugs & Other Thugs*. Pownal, VT: Storey Publishing, 1971.

Indian Cookbook. Ardmore, OK: Ardmore Indian Bicentennial Committee, 1975.

James, Wilma Roberts. *Know Your Poisonous Plants*. Healdsburg, CA: Naturegraph Publishers, 1973.

Kennedy, Paul E. *American Wildflowers*. New York: Dover Publications, 1971.

Kunz, George Frederick. *The Curious Lore of Precious Stones*. New York: Dover Publications, 1970.

Llewellyn's Moon Sign Book. St. Paul, MN: Llewellyn Publishing Company, 1986.

Marks, Geoffrey, and William K. Beatty. *The Medical Garden*. New York: Charles Scribner's Sons, 1971.

McClelland, Elizabeth A. *Small Animals of North America*. New York: Dover Publications, 1981.

Mecco Barbecue & Smoker Cookbook. Birmingham, AL: Marketlink Custom Publishing, 1993.

Meyer, Clarence. *The Herbalist Almanac*. Glenwood, IL: Meyerbooks, 1977.

Meyers, Chet, and Al Lindner. *Catching Fish*. Minneapolis, MN: Dillon Press, 1981.

Miller, Richard Alan. *The Magical and Ritual Use of Herbs*. New York: Destiny Books, 1983.

Millspaugh, Charles F. *American Medicinal Plants*. New York: Dover Publications, 1974.

Nichol, John. *Bites & Stings: The World of Venomous Animals*. New York: Facts on File, Inc., 1989.

Pyrom, J. *Frogs & Toads*. Neptune City, NJ: T.F.H. Publications, Inc., n.d.

Riotte, Louise. *Astrological Gardening*. Pownal, VT: Storey Publishing, 1989.

____. *Carrots Love Tomatoes*. Pownal, VT: Storey Publishing, 1975.

____. *The Complete Guide to Growing Berries and Grapes*. Dallas, TX: Taylor Publishing Co., 1993.

____. *The Complete Guide To Growing Nuts*. Dallas, TX: Taylor Publishing Co., 1993.

____. *In Nature's Hands*. Dallas, TX: Taylor Publishing Co., 1992.

____. *Planetary Planting*. San Diego, CT: Astro Computer Services, 1982.

____. *Sleeping With A Sunflower*. Pownal, VT: Storey Publishing, 1986.

____. *Successful Small Food Gardens*. Pownal, VT: Storey Publishing, 1993.

Rose, Jeanne. *Herbs and Things*. New York: Putnam Publishing Co., 1972.

Sukumaran, Dr. N. *Frog Farming*. Fisheries College, Tamil Nadu Agricultural University, Tuticorin, India, n.d.

Sweet, Muriel. *Common Edible and Useful Plants of the West*. Healdsburg, CA: Naturegraph Publishers, 1976.

Tompkins, Peter, and Christopher Bird. *The Secret Life of Plants*. New York: Avon Books, 1973.

Allen, J.S., and A.C. Lopinot. *Small Lakes and Ponds: Their Construction and Care.* Springfield, IL: Illinois Department of Conservation, n.d.

Beem, Marley. *Crawfish and Crawfish Farming — An Introduction for 4-H.* Stillwater, OK: Cooperative Extension Service, Division of Aquaculture, Oklahoma State University, n.d.

_____. *Getting Started in Aquaculture.* Stillwater, OK: Cooperative Extension Service, Division of Aquaculture, Oklahoma State University, n.d.

_____. *Grass Carp for Pond Weed Management.* Stillwater, OK: Cooperative Extension Service, Division of Aquaculture, Oklahoma State University, n.d.

Commercial Alternative Aquaculture Newsline, Third Floor Courthouse, McAlester, OK 74501.

Dillard, J.G. *Missouri Pond Handbook.* Jefferson City, MO: Missouri Department of Conservation (P.O. Box 180, Jefferson City, MO 65101), n.d.

Durborow, Robert M., and Craig S. Tucker. *Aquatic Weed Control in Catfish Ponds.* Frankfort, KY: Cooperative Extension Program, Kentucky State University, n.d.

Federal Emergency Management Agency. *Answers to Questions About the National Flood Insurance Program.*

Lopinot, A.C. *Pond Fish and Fishing in Illinois.* Fishery Bulletin No. 5, Illinois Department of Conservation (Springfield, IL 62706).

Kansas Department of Wildlife and Parks. *Producing Fish and Wildlife from Kansas Ponds* (R.R. 2, Box 54-A, Pratt, KS 67124).

National Flood Insurance Program, *Flood Map Distribution Center,* 6930 (A-P), San Tomas Road, Baltimore, Maryland 21227-6227.

Lichtkopper, Frank R. *Factors to Consider in Establishing Successful Aquaculture Businesses in the North Central Region.* North Central Regional Aquaculture Center, Michigan State University (13 Natural Resources Bldg., East Lansing, MI 48824-1222).

OSU Extension Service. *Catfish Farming.* Stillwater, OK: Oklahoma State University, n.d.

Shelton, James L., and Tim R. Murphy. *Aquatic Weed Management.* Beltsville, MD: Southern Regional Aquaculture Center, n.d.

Soil Conservation Office, U.S. Department of Agriculture. *Building a Pond.* Farmer's Bulletin No. 2256.

_____. *Warm Water Fish Ponds.* Farmer's Bulletin No. 2250.

_____. *Ponds for Water Supply and Recreation.* Agriculture Handbook No. 387.

U.S. Govt. Printing Office, *Gem Stones of the United States.* Survey Bulletin 1042-G.

Wellborn, Thomas L. *Channel Catfish, Life History and Biology.* Beltsville, MD: Southern Regional Aquaculture Center, n.d.

Whitley, James R., with Barbara Bassett, J. G. Dillard, and Rebecca A. Haefner. *Water Plants for Missouri Ponds.* Fish and Wildlife Division, Missouri Department of Conservation (2901 W. Truman Blvd., P.O. Box 180, Jefferson City, MO 65102-0180).

The following publications can be ordered from the Aquaculture Information Center, National Aquacultural Library, Beltsville, Maryland 20705-2351:

McVey, Eileen M., *Feeds & Feeding of Catfish*

Beem, Marley, *Aquaculture: Realities and Potentials When Getting Started*

Wellborn, Thomas L., *Site Selection of Levee-Type Fish Production Ponds*

Murphy, Tim R. and Shelton, James L., *Channel Catfish — Dietary Effects on Body Composition & Storage Quality*

Wellborn, Thomas L., *Aquatic Weed Management*

Masser, Michael and Jenson, John W., *Calculating Area & Volume of Ponds and Tanks*

Buttner, Joseph, Soderborg, Richard W., and Terlizzi, Daniel E., *An Introduction To Water Chemistry in Freshwater Aquaculture*

Jensen, Gary L., Bankston, Joseph D., and Jensen, John W., *Pond Aeration, Pub. 370;* also *Types & Uses of Aeration Equipment, Pub. 371*

The following publications may be ordered from the Consumer Information Center, N, P.O. Box 100, Pueblo, Colorado 81002:

In the Event of a Flood (What to do during a flood and how to minimize loss of life and property)

In Time of Emergency (Advice on protecting life, health, and property from natural and man-made disasters)

Research Assistance

The Samuel Roberts Noble Foundation, P.O. Box 2480, 2510 Highway 199, East Ardmore, Oklahoma 73401

Suppliers

Applewood Seed Company
5380 Vivian Street
Arvada, CO 89992
Wildflower seeds for all areas.

Avon Products
9 West 57th Street
New York, NY 10019
Skin-So-Soft (works as mosquito repellent).

Dunn's Fish Farm
Fittstown, OK
800-433-2950; 405-777-2202
24-hour phone service.

Gurney's Seed and Nursery Co.
110 Capital Street
Yankton, SD 57079
Ground covers, plants, and trees.

W. G. F. Kester's Nursery
P.O. Box 516
Omro, WI 54163
Water plants, including arrowhead, pickerelweed, bulrush.

Lilypons Water Gardens
P.O. Box 10
Buckeystown, MD 21717-0010
Water lilies, fish, pool equipment.

Park Seed Company, Inc.
Cokesbury Road
Greenwood, SC 29647-0001
Wildflower seeds, plants.

Patio Garden Ponds
P.O. Box 890402
Oklahoma City, OK 73189-0402
Pre-formed ponds, filters, water lilies, water plants.

Plants of the Southwest
1570 Pacheco Street
Santa Fe, NM 87501
Wildflower seeds for the Southwest. A wide variety of habitats.

Polytank, Inc.
R.R. 1, Box 13
Litchfield, MN 55355
Fish hatchery tank and other supplies.

Rainbow Plastics Filter Division
P.O. Box 4127
El Monte, CA 91734
Aquaculture and mariculture water treatment systems.

Tenax Corporation
8291 Patuxent Range Road
Jessup, MD 20794
Plastic nets and grids for construction of cages, traps, and barriers.

Wayside Gardens
Hodges, SC 29695-0001
Ferns, iris.

Welp, Inc.
P.O. Box 77
Bancroft, IA 50517-9977
Ducks, geese, Cornish hens, chickens, equipment; will ship to all 50 states.

INDEX

Page references in *italics* indicate illustrations.